A NATION REBORN

A NATION REBORN

Britain's role in Israel's restoration

Charles Gardner

Christian Publications International

First published in Great Britain by
Christian Publications International
an imprint of
Buy Research Ltd.
PO Box 212 SAFFRON WALDEN CB10 2UU

Cover design by Justyn Hall at J8 Creative
Email: justyn@J8creative.co.uk

Cover photograph – Dead Sea from Masada, Israel,
Copyright ©Deena Gainor 2016
www.dgainor.com

www.christian-publications-int.com

ISBN 978-0-9926674-9-8

Printed in England by Imprint Digital, Exeter
and worldwide by CreateSpace

The author's passion, breadth of knowledge and understanding shines through this book. Its thoroughly biblical content is backed up by clear summaries of historical context along with personal and anecdotal accounts to add colour to the text. The significance of the Jewish people – past, present and future – is framed within the glorious prospect of the coming reign of Messiah as the fullness of His kingdom is ushered in. There's plenty here for the reader prayerfully to ponder, reflect on and perhaps respond to.

Ray Lockhart
Vice-president of CMJ (Church's Ministry among the Jewish people), former Israel Director and Rector of Christ Church, Jerusalem, 1991–1999.

Charles has contributed articles to our global news service for many years, so I am very familiar with his sharp, succinct style that takes readers to the heart of the matter on a number of hot topical issues, especially the Middle East. I highly recommend this inspiring book on such a vitally important subject. Everyone should read it.

Dan Wooding
Founder and chief editor of ASSIST News Service

A magnificent book and a most important work which deserves to be widely read – top of my list for anyone wanting to know about Israel.

Christopher Proudlove
Journalist

This book is well-researched and informative. It sets out historical facts, looks at how great men of God believed in the return of the Jews to Israel and explains scriptural truths in an interesting and easy-to-understand format. It would be ideal both for those who want facts at their fingertips and those who simply want to know what right Israel has to exist. It deserves to be a winner!

Pam Smith
Methodist local preacher and founder of Methodist Friends of Israel

Contents

ACKNOWLEDGEMENTS

This book is dedicated to Jewish people everywhere. My hope and prayer is that they will come to know just how high, and wide, and long, and deep, is the love of God. I wish also to thank my wonderful wife, Linda, for her encouragement, and the many others who have inspired me to write about these momentous times. I think particularly of Martin and Margaret Hall, Owen Hoskin, Theresa Newell, Ryan Jones, Clifford Hill, Frances Rabbitts and Clifford Denton. And I am also most grateful to Pam Smith and Ray Lockhart for their painstaking appraisal of my manuscript, and to John Scriven and the publishers for their tremendous support.

FOREWORD

I wholeheartedly endorse this book! One might wonder if there is a place for another book on Israel, its history, legitimacy and rebirth, but I believe that this offering will find its place, bringing fresh perspectives. This is especially so because it has the feel of the work of a journalist – clearly written and with that journalistic pace touching very much on items of news. Yet it also digs deeply and has a vast width. It is informative, anecdotal, very much evangelistic and also prophetically challenging. I would hope that it would find itself in the hands of people of influence in our nation to steer them towards thinking again, as well as in the hands of many others in Church and nation. I found no points of disagreement historically, biblically or prophetically and I was also introduced to some information that is quite new to me.

Clifford Denton
Author, Hebraic teacher and *Prophecy Today* Chairman

PREFACE

The purpose of this book is to inform, inspire and challenge readers over what is perhaps the most significant event of our times both from a political and spiritual perspective. As Britain has recently marked the centenary of its own promise to restore the Jews to their ancient homeland, I look at how it all came about and what it means for us today. In particular, it is both a celebration of Britain's positive role in the matter of Jewish restoration and a call to repentance for broken pledges and downright anti-Semitism. At a time when Israel gets a generally bad press from both East and West, this is also an attempt to bring balance and truth on the subject to a media world awash with politically-correct propaganda. I am aware, too, that other nations – particularly the United States of America – have also played a significant part in Jewish restoration, but I leave their story to another book, and perhaps another author. Even South Africa, my own country, has played its part. On a recent visit to the Diaspora Museum in Tel Aviv, I discovered there was a Jewish community in Cape Town in the very early years of its settlement by the Dutch East India Company, and that by 1669 – just 17 years after its founding – two members of that community had become followers of Jesus.

INTRODUCTION

Armageddon Ahead!

When President Trump made good on his election promise to recognise Jerusalem as Israel's capital, it triggered a political earthquake. And yet he was only facing facts. Jerusalem has Jewish connections going back over 3,000 years, and any competing claim is no more than fiction. But in joining the chorus of disapproval for the USA move, Britain has further betrayed a pledge she made over a hundred years ago.

But this book is not all bad news; it is also a celebration of the inestimable privilege we enjoyed in paving the way for the restoration to their ancient land of the Jewish people. Sadly, however, the UK government didn't quite complete their God-given task, and international mandate, as they succumbed to constant appeasement of those who oppose Jewish aspirations. As a result, we have blood on our hands and are in ever-increasing danger of falling under the judgment reserved for nations refusing to serve God's chosen race. (See Joel 3.2.) Isaiah writes: "For the nation or kingdom that will not serve you will perish; it will be utterly ruined" (Isa 60.12).

The US Congress voted to recognise Jerusalem as Israel's capital in 1995, but successive Presidents have simply put off implementing the decision until now.

Even Arab commentators are encouraging their people to accept reality. Saudi academic Abdulhameed Hakeem says they need to recognise Jerusalem's sanctity to Jews.[1] And he has also stressed that Israel and Saudi Arabia face a common Nazi-like threat in Iran,[2] which has reportedly pledged every assistance to terror group Hamas in "the battle for the defence of Jerusalem".[3]

With its efforts to make good on a long-promised boast to wipe Israel off the map, Iran continues to be a serious threat (despite popular protests from within the rogue regime).

So with the nations as a whole setting their face against Israel, and denying their right both to the land and their capital, the stage is being set for the battle of the ages which, according to the Bible, will take place at Armageddon (or the plain of Jezreel) in northern Israel (Revelation 16.16). But the trigger will be the status of Jerusalem. (See Zechariah 12.2f.)

Elijah of old was engaged in a great battle with 400 false prophets in this same region. (See 1 Kings 18). It was a bloody contest – all the false prophets were subsequently slaughtered – and took place on Mt Carmel which, as it happens, overlooks Armageddon.

It may come as a surprise to some that Jerusalem is God's very own city – he effectively owns it; it bears his name. (See Daniel 9.18f & Nehemiah 1.9) But false deities, with the connivance of numerous world powers, refuse to acknowledge this.

Jesus lamented over Jerusalem because of the people's rejection of him, but at the same time prophesied their ultimate acceptance of his rule (see Matthew 23.39). He has not finished with Jerusalem; he will come back just as he left (Acts 1.11).

Yet despite all the evidence supporting Israel's claim, including a heap of archaeological finds, Palestinian leaders refuse to accept the truth. In the year 2000, Yasser Arafat turned down the chance of a comprehensive peace deal because he refused to recognise Jewish historical ties to Jerusalem's Temple Mount. "The Jews never had a Temple at the site," he said at the time.[4] The entire Palestinian narrative is based on a lie that would be recognised by children at kindergarten – yet world leaders don't get it!

But they must get used to the idea. That there would be an almighty battle over the territory was always part of the script. But Elohim (God) will be the ultimate victor, "watching over his word to perform it" (Jeremiah 1.12).

The Messiah is waiting for that day – and I pray it will come soon – when his ancient people greet him once more with gladness, saying: "Blessed is he who comes in the name of the Lord!" (Matthew 23.39, Psalm 118.26)

Meanwhile Israel has passed the hugely significant milestone of 70 years since its rebirth. This is the same period of time that the Jews were exiled in Babylon from 586 BC, and the same prophets who foretold their return from all the nations to which they were later dispersed wrote that they would first come back to their ancient land, and then return to their Lord. In other words, their physical return would be followed by a spiritual restoration when they would recognise Jesus (Yeshua in Hebrew) as their Messiah. The return from Babylon was followed by re-dedication to God in tandem with the rebuilding of Jerusalem.

Notes

[1] *Jerusalem Post*, quoted by *JNN* 22 December 2017.

[2] Ibid.

[3] *Times of Israel*, quoted by *United with Israel* 28 December 2017

[4] Christian Friends of Israel's *Watching Over Zion* newsletter 30 November 2017.

Chapter 1

Legacy of a Nineteenth Century Prophet

Tucked away in a beautifully tranquil part of Suffolk, noted among art enthusiasts everywhere as Constable Country,[1] is an ancient stone church dating back 700 years. There is nothing particularly unusual about that in England, where the sight of a glorious steeple piercing the sky through a canopy of trees is the focus of nearly every village. But I was especially drawn to this one, on the edge of the magnificent Helmingham Hall estate belonging to Lord and Lady Tollemache, whose fabulous gardens we had just visited.

It turns out that this aristocratic family has had strong connections with the church over the centuries and had been responsible for the mass of illuminated Bible verses inscribed on virtually every spare space inside the building.

Anyone who comes to church without a Bible has much of it "printed in large type" on the walls, while the pulpit is graphically backed up by the text "Woe to me if I do not preach the gospel!"

Intrigued to find out more of its history, I soon discovered that none other than John Charles Ryle (later to become the first Bishop of Liverpool) was Rector there for nearly 20 years in the mid-19th century (1844-1861).

But J C Ryle (as he was generally known) would in no way have been intimidated by such evangelical fervour. He would literally have basked in it like a sun-seeker soaking up the warmth of its rays.

During his time at Helmingham, he wrote over eighty tracts which were delivered to every door in the parish.

He challenged the complacency of many who seemed uninterested in their spiritual state with prose that – unusually for the day – was both pithy and engaging. He mocked the notion that you should be thought very uncharitable if you dared to question whether a man was a Christian, thus:

> The man's practice may be no better than that of a heathen: many a respectable Hindu might put him to shame – but what of that? He is an Englishman. He has been baptized. He goes to church, and behaves decently when there. What more would you have?[2]

He reminded his readers that "sacraments, services and sermons may produce outward formality, and clothe us with a skin of religion, but there will be no life." Only the Holy Spirit could wake us from our spiritual slumber and save us from the "deep corruption" of our human nature. He is particularly mindful of those who profess Christianity without backing it up by a transformed life:

> Sin is plainly not considered their worst enemy, nor the Lord Jesus their best friend, nor the will of God their rule of life, nor salvation the great end of their existence.

Urging us to receive the Spirit, he concludes:

> You may not like the tidings. You may call it enthusiasm, or fanaticism, or extravagance. I take my stand on the plain teaching of the Bible.

Unlike some today, he emphasises that Christ is the "only way" to heaven and mocks those who treat the Bible as "a heathen idol" only to be brought out at christenings, or upon the arrival of sickness, the doctor and death.

His messages are urgent, passionate, blunt and uncompromising – and what a legacy he has left, for he still speaks, even though dead. He continues to be widely read (a fresh autobiography was published as recently as 2016),[3] and there are apparently many Internet websites devoted to him.

Oh that today's bishops would speak with such directness and authority! With some notable exceptions, they seem to have had what many have dubbed "the operation" to remove their spine.

But Ryle's passion for the gospel echoes down the ages, still addressing those lost in a sea of despair, confusion and hopelessness: "I fear lest you should live without Christ, die without pardon, rise again without hope, receive judgment without mercy, and sink into hell without remedy."

He was unequivocal in stating that "the Bible is all true, and must be fulfilled". And so he firmly believed that the Jews scattered around the world for 18 centuries would soon return to their ancient homeland in fulfilment of many scriptures. And he encouraged Christians to work and pray toward that end. He said:

> I believe that the Jews shall ultimately be gathered again as a separate nation, restored to their own land and turned to the faith of Christ (Messiah).

And so it was, less than 50 years after he died in 1900, that the modern State of Israel was born! And a growing number of its people have since acknowledged Jesus as their Messiah.

Judge for yourself whether you think a man with such foresight was off the mark in diagnosing the spiritual health of his parishioners.

He did not escape suffering himself – he was twice widowed while at Helmingham – but was not afraid to preach what many today would deem "hell-fire and damnation" as he left his readers with this fiery challenge: "Where is the man that can hold his finger for a minute in the flame of a candle? Who shall dwell with everlasting burnings?"

That there was a heaven to be gained and a hell to be shunned was a fairly orthodox line taken by preachers of the day, but few even then had the courage to put it quite as bluntly as J C Ryle.

Thus galvanised by the gospel, Ryle lit a flame that time would not extinguish and my prayer is that readers will continue to have their hearts similarly warmed by fire from heaven.

Evangelical revival stirs hope for Israel

Although the past century has not been Britain's finest hour with respect to her dealings with the Jewish people, many are unaware of the very positive role she had previously played towards Israel's restoration. And it was only because of a revival of biblical knowledge and understanding led by evangelical Christians that the pathway was opened at all. Even politicians and military leaders with insight into the Scriptures could see that God's eventual purpose for his chosen people was that they return to their ancient homeland from which they had been dispersed to the four corners of the earth by their Roman conquerors nearly 2,000 years earlier. In an era when Britain led the world, ruling the waves over an empire on which the sun never set, successive governments were strongly influenced by the Victorian tendency to put God at the centre of national life. And it was not a coincidence that UK missionaries took the gospel around the globe.

So it was hardly surprising that the men in power often bowed to a higher authority than their own, giving great weight to the promises of Scripture which they held to be inerrant. All of which, in God's perfect timing, coincided with the rise of Zionism when Jewish leaders began to campaign for a national home, as a result of which Jews began returning to the land of their forefathers in sizeable numbers from the 1880s. So it was that, in 1917, the British Government's so-called Balfour Declaration pledged to do all it could towards this end. A letter published in the *Jerusalem Post* on Armistice Sunday 1994 reflects an understanding of just how important it was: "I think the time has come to make up with the British and to restore the friendship of the Balfour Days, without which there would have been no State of Israel..."

But evangelical Christians had never seen Israel's restoration as merely a physical return to their ancient homeland, because the prophets had also repeatedly spoken of a return to the God of Israel. The general sense of prophetic timing indicated that such spiritual renewal would come in the wake of this great latter-day immigration in the same way that the Law of Moses was only given after they were saved out of Egypt.

Jesus told Nicodemus, a Jewish religious leader, that, "no-one can see the kingdom of God unless he is born again", and, "no-one can enter the kingdom of God unless he is born of water and the Spirit" (See John chapter 3). Serious students of Scripture look for the great day of revelation when Jewish people as a whole will finally know, love and welcome the Lamb of God who shed his blood for them as he paid the ultimate penalty for our sins on a cross outside Jerusalem's Old City walls 2,000 years ago. The Scriptures also tell us that Israel's dual return – which we are witnessing today with nearly half of world Jewry back in the land, and rapidly growing numbers of so-called Messianic believers (Jews who have accepted Jesus as Messiah) – will be accompanied by the final conflict of the ages in anticipation of Christ's long-promised Second Coming.

Bishop Ryle's challenging style would no doubt be seen by some as way too harsh in these days of political correctness, but he was far from alone – especially among those perceived at the time as evangelical giants. Nowadays, even Christians seem to think cosying up to a left-wing view of things is the fashionable and acceptable thing to do, especially on matters of Israel, now a modern state, in fulfilment of the ancient Scriptures, constantly battling for survival amid attacks (by rockets, bombs, knives and guns), which are repeatedly flung her way by terrorists and enemy states.

Notes

[1] John Constable was a Suffolk-born English romantic painter known principally for his landscape paintings of Dedham Vale, the area surrounding his home – now known as "Constable Country".

[2] This and other quotes are taken from various pamphlets published in 1855 by J C Ryle under the title *Plain Speaking* (second series) and freely available from Helmingham Parish Church (St Mary's), with additional biographical notes from Rev Dr Alan Munden of Newcastle-upon-Tyne.

[3] *Bishop J C Ryle's Autobiography – the Early Years*, published by Banner of Truth, edited by Andrew Atherstone.

Chapter 2

Evangelical Christians: Consistent Friends of Israel

A controversial church leader has once again heightened divisions among the people of Britain about the place of Israel in God's purposes. Rev Stephen Sizer, a Church of England vicar from a wealthy part of Surrey, reportedly posted a link to an article on Facebook blaming Israel for the 9/11 attacks on the United States. Fortunately, it seems that the Church for once took action by investigating the issue, with a spokesman saying it was a matter of "deep sorrow and shame" that the posts appeared in the same week as the 70th anniversary of the liberation of Auschwitz.

Rev Sizer, who is certainly not representative of all Brits, later removed the link and apologised for his "ill-considered and misguided" actions. But the real mystery of his position, which many UK churchgoers find so hard to understand, is that he is widely described as an "Evangelical Christian" (those who see the Bible as the final authority on all matters).

For while the history of Britain's dealings with the Jewish people over the centuries is by no means covered in glory, the truth is that its Evangelical Christian community, who have had an influence on the world out of all proportion to their numbers, have been consistent friends of Israel – seeing clearly from the plain meaning of the written Word of God that those who bless them will themselves be blessed (Genesis 12.3) and that those who curse them will face judgment.

Evangelicalism produced such spiritual giants as John and

Charles Wesley, William Wilberforce, Charles Simeon and Bishop J C Ryle (all of whom were members of the Church of England – the established church) along with legendary Baptist preacher Charles Spurgeon. Their influence on changing hearts and lives, both practically and spiritually, over the centuries is incalculable as they helped restore kindness, godliness and gentleness to a nation that might otherwise have gone down the same route as France under the 1789 Revolution.

Not far away from where I live is the ancient city of York, which witnessed the massacre of its entire Jewish community (estimated at 150) on March 16 1190 as part of a wave of anti-Semitism across Europe, paving the way for the expulsion of Jews from Britain altogether 100 years later.

But it was thanks in part to the rise of Evangelicals in the 17th century that Jews were invited back, and they have been blessing Britain ever since with their unique blend of innovation, ingenuity and entrepreneurial skills. The so-called 'Pilgrim Fathers', who went out from this area of England to help found the United States of America, apparently persuaded Oliver Cromwell (leader of the short-lived republic) to re-open its doors to the Jewish people.

Wilberforce, who was also from Yorkshire and who is most famously known for the passing in 1807 of the Abolition of Slavery Bill following a lifelong campaign in the British Parliament, was one of the founders of the Church's Ministry among the Jews (CMJ) which still exists today as a global society dedicated to the spiritual renewal of God's people. CMJ were initially responding to the need of thousands of Jewish immigrants from the pogroms of Russia, reaching out to them with the love of God – as the Bible tells us to do. The society was subsequently at the forefront of efforts to persuade the British Government to facilitate the establishment of a homeland in the Middle East for the Jewish people. This resulted in the so-called Balfour Declaration of 1917 and became a practical possibility just weeks later when General Allenby's forces took Jerusalem from the Turks.

Britain was to betray the Jews yet again as it sought to appease Arab demands but, in the end, God's precious people got their land back (or some of it, at least) – more than partly thanks to the Evangelicals of England, who were convinced that the Bible means what it says. For Holy Writ had clearly stated that, after a period of dispersal throughout the nations, Jewish people would return to their ancient land from every corner of the globe.

I was so thrilled when I read that the Israeli government has launched what amounts to a national Bible Study. A return to the Scriptures always brought revival to the land in ancient times, and will do so again. The Word of God has all the answers to the elusive peace for which politicians seek. Would it not be wonderful if Britain and other nations followed this lead, ceased their pathetic idolatry of a mish-mash of religions and ideologies, and returned to the God of Israel, who alone is God! The great "I am" has spoken through the Bible.

Legendary preachers back Israel

As early as 1649, when preaching before the House of Commons, John Owen, regarded as the greatest theologian of the English Puritan movement, spoke of "the bringing home of his ancient people to be one fold with the fullness of the Gentiles… in answer to millions of prayers put up at the throne of grace for this very glory, in all generations."

John Wesley, possibly England's greatest Christian leader, spoke of Israel's restoration a century before Ryle. In his notes on Romans, the Methodist founder wrote: "So many prophecies refer to this grand event that it is surprising any

Christian can doubt of it. And these are greatly confirmed by the wonderful preservation of the Jews as a distinct people to this day." And he was not alone. In the 1780s, Baptist minister James Bicheno, in his book *Signs of the Times*, argued that the upheaval in Europe was a beginning of the "end of days" foretold in the Bible, and a precursor to the return of Jesus, and that part of the lead-up to this great event would be a restoration of his own people to their biblical homeland along with a subsequent national spiritual revival.

It is well known that Wesley was much influenced by the Moravians.[1] In fact, it was their shining Christian witness that led to his conversion in 1738. It was around this time that Moravian Johann Dober pioneered Jewish mission in the Netherlands where he came to be much loved in Amsterdam's Jewish quarter as 'Rabbi Schmuel'. A brilliant man, who was master of the Hebrew tongue and expert in Jewish customs, he apparently never tried to prove that Christ was the Messiah of the scriptural prophecies, but simply told, in a kindly way, how Jesus had risen from the dead and shared their hope of a national gathering in Palestine.

In 1797, Thomas Witherby, commenting on a book *The Restoration of the Jews – the crisis of all nations*, said he felt confident that "England, under a new Cyrus, would be chosen to perform God's purposes of mercy towards Israel." (Cyrus was the Persian king who allowed the Jews taken into captivity to return home and rebuild Jerusalem). This and many other nuggets of information was recorded in a little-known 1956 book, *The Vision was There*, written by Franz Kobler, a non-Christian, Jewish author, who wrote in his introduction: "Nowhere more than in Britain has the idea of the restoration of Israel been developed into a doctrine and become the object of a movement extending over more than three centuries… It is in fact one of the rare instances of the continuous interest shown by one nation in the destiny of another." In the 1840s, he added, Charles Henry Churchill, ancestor of Sir Winston, spoke and wrote of England's bonding with the Jewish nation and, at an important public meeting, stated that "God has put into my heart the desire to serve his ancient people". A very significant book on the subject was *The coming of Messiah in glory and majesty*, written in Spanish by a South American Roman Catholic priest, Emanuel Lacunza. It was translated into English and published in London in 1827, with a long preliminary discourse by Edward Irving, an early pioneer of Pentecostalism.

In 1839 the Church of Scotland sent a delegation, including Robert Murray McCheyne, to the Holy Land on a mission of enquiry. On his return, McCheyne preached a sermon in Dundee on 'Our duty to Israel' in which he said: "The greatest glory and joy anyone can experience is to be like God, and to care first for the Jews is to be like God... The whole Bible shows that God has a special affection for Israel..."

Charles Spurgeon, the so-called 'Prince of Preachers', speaking of the restoration of the Jews at Southwark Cathedral in 1855, said: "We do not think enough of it. But certainly, if there is anything promised in the Bible, it is this. You cannot read the Bible without seeing clearly that there is to be an actual restoration of the Children of Israel... The day shall yet come when the Jews, who were the first Apostles to the Gentiles, the first missionaries to us, who were far off, shall be gathered in again. Until that shall be, the fullness of the church's glory can never come."

And Bishop Ryle, to whom I have already referred, again spoke plainly on the subject in a sermon delivered in London in May 1868, declaring: "However great the difficulties surrounding many parts of unfulfilled prophecy, two points appear to my own mind to stand out as plainly as if written by a sunbeam. One of these points is the second personal advent of our Lord Jesus Christ before the Millennium. The other of these points is the future literal gathering of the Jewish nation, and their restoration to their own land."

He went on to say, "Out of the sixteen prophets of the Old Testament, there are at least ten in which the gathering and restoration of the Jews in the latter days are expressly mentioned." He followed this with a quotation from each of those ten prophets, and concluded: "I believe there is one common remark that applies to them all. They all point to a time which is yet future. They all predict the final gathering of the Jewish nation from the four quarters of the globe, and their restoration to their own land... I ask you, then, to settle it firmly in your mind, that when God says a thing shall be done, we ought to believe it."

Chinese pilgrims flock to UK town

In the 21st century, meanwhile, coach tours are being conducted around a UK town, not far from where I live, to enable Chinese pilgrims to pay tribute to one of their greatest heroes.

James Hudson Taylor, who was also a true friend of Israel, was born in Barnsley, Yorkshire, in 1832 and later followed the call of God to China, where he established hundreds of churches and nearly 200 schools. As founder of the China Inland Mission (now Overseas Missionary Fellowship), he became spiritual father to millions of Chinese Christians. As part of their weekly *Songs of Praise* programme, BBC Television focused on the visit to Barnsley of a coach-load of British-based Chinese tourists. Interviewed about what Taylor meant to them and filmed publicly praying and thanking God for his ministry, they sang *Amazing Grace* in their native tongue as they honoured his memory. "I cannot believe God has used this little place (population 225,000) to do an amazing work among the Chinese," one of the tourists told the BBC. Historian Ruth Tucker wrote: "No other missionary in the 19 centuries since the Apostle Paul has had a wider vision and has carried out a more systematised plan of evangelising a broad geographical area than Hudson Taylor."

So what was the secret of his success? Firm resolve to follow a clear calling was no doubt a key – he was so determined to identify with the Chinese that he adopted their dress and even wore a pigtail. But despite his primary calling to China, he clearly also saw the priority Scripture set on Jewish evangelism; that even for the Apostle Paul, who was called primarily to the Gentiles, the gospel was "to the Jew first" (Romans 1.16). Taylor was so convinced of this truth that, in his latter years, he would write out a cheque in support of a Jewish mission on the first day of each year.

This habit began on New Year's Day 1897 when, at home in Britain, he went round to the house of one John Wilkinson, founder of the Mildmay Mission to the Jews,[2] with what Taylor's wife Jennie[3] described as "a brotherly note enclosing a gift". A cheque was accompanied by a note saying "To the Jew first". Mrs Taylor continued: "Mr Wilkinson's warm heart was touched, and he immediately wrote a brotherly reply, enclosing his own cheque for the same amount, with the words: 'And also to the Gentile'. This helpful interchange of sympathy was kept up ever after,"[4] she wrote, "the only change being that each doubled the amount of their contribution. Work among God's ancient people occupied a special place in the prayerful sympathy of both Mr and Mrs Taylor," she explained.[5]

St Paul wrote: "I am not ashamed of the gospel, because it is the power of God for the salvation of everyone who believes: first for the Jew, then for the Gentile" (Romans 1.16). This statement reflects something of God's heart for the Jewish people, first expressed in Genesis 12.3 as: "I will bless those who bless you..."

Taylor's attitude and understanding of the place in God's heart for the Jews will surely have contributed in no small measure to the incredible success of his mission – there are at least as many Christians in China today as there are people in the UK! And that is despite severe persecution. Now Chinese Christians are working on a plan to take the gospel all the way back to Jerusalem, where it all started!

The most encouraging aspect of watching those Chinese believers paying tribute to Hudson Taylor was that they represented the undeniable evidence that what you sow, you will surely reap. As St Paul urged the Galatians: "Let us not become weary in well doing, for in due season we shall reap a harvest if we do not give up" (Gal 6.9).

Another leading 19th century evangelical, Charles Simeon, was similarly convinced about Jewish restoration. On one occasion, when waxing lyrical with his visions of a return of the Jews to Christ ushering in worldwide revival, a friend passed a note to him stating, "Six million of Jews and 600 millions [*sic*] of Gentiles – which is more important?"[6] (This was clearly a reference to the Jews representing 1% of the world's population at the time. The figure today is just 0.1%).

Simeon scribbled back, "If the conversion of the six is to be life from the dead to the 600, what then?" (He was referring to Romans 11.15.) The Jews were the key, he was saying. The gospel is for the Jew first!

Notes

[1] The Moravian Church, one of the world's oldest denominations, significantly influenced England's 18th century evangelical revival.
[2] The mission is now known as Messianic Testimony following a 1977 merger with the Hebrew Christian Testimony to Israel.
[3] Jennie was Taylor's second wife. His first wife, Maria, died in 1870 of cholera, just days after losing her sixth child, Noel, in infancy.
[4] Taylor died in 1905.
[5] I am indebted to Saltshakers.com, the website of author Steve Maltz, for this insight into Taylor's love for the Jews.
[6] See my book *Peace in Jerusalem*, olivepresspublisher.com

Chapter 3

Prophetic Significance of Jewish Home-Call

As with so much that is spiritual, the mainstream media largely missed the significance of Israeli Prime Minister Binyamin (Bibi) Netanyahu's call for Jews to come home in the wake of a significant upsurge of anti-Semitism in Europe. His assurance of welcome for what could amount to a mass migration of some seven million, virtually doubling the nation's population, came in the wake of the wave of terror attacks in European cities in which Jews have been key targets. If heeded, it would represent one of the most awesome events in history, fulfilling many Scriptures in the process.

But the call is not so much political, as Bibi's detractors suggest, as prophetic. As I have already said, Evangelical Christians – those who believe in the absolute authority of the Bible and who have been consistent friends of Israel over the centuries – generally see the rebirth of Israel in 1948 as the fulfilment of ancient prophecies by Isaiah, Jeremiah, Ezekiel and others, which is why they have prayed and proclaimed these truths into existence.

They also know that the prophecies of return have a twofold application – first, the natural (a return to the Land), then the spiritual (a return to the Lord). Jeremiah writes of a 'new covenant' through which God's people will all know the Lord (Jer 31) while Ezekiel writes of a 'new heart' and 'new spirit' and of a 'heart of flesh' replacing a heart of stone following the return to their ancient homeland of Jews from every corner of the globe (Ezek 36). Zechariah even talks of national repentance and mourning at the appearance in Jerusalem of their Messiah.

So the end-time schedule goes something like this: Jews from every nation return to their homeland after nearly 2,000 years of dispersion and persecution. Then, when they are safely back in the Land, they are finally restored into a relationship with the One who chose them as His special, treasured possession and the 'apple of His eye'.

The scene has been set by the Israeli government's launch of a national Bible study, encouraging every citizen to search the Scriptures, to rediscover their roots and find hope instead of despair, faith instead of fear and peace instead of war. I believe such a study – among other factors – will open eyes to the nature and reality of Israel's hope – the Messiah. Psalm 119.105 puts it like this: "Your word is a lamp to my feet and a light for my path."

Denmark's chief rabbi, Jair Melchior, says, "terror is not a reason to move to Israel". But this is to ignore the many historic precedents which saw those making Aliyah (immigrating) doing so not simply out of love for Israel and Zionism, but because it represents a safe haven. After all, the modern state rose from the ashes of the Holocaust which, as Mr Netanyahu has stated, represents a fulfilment of Ezekiel's dry bones prophecy (chapter 37). In fact, it was after being beaten up by anti-Semite thugs in the heart of Europe that Mr Netanyahu's grandfather promised, if he survived, to take his family to the Jewish homeland.

What is more, Israel's first Prime Minister, David Ben-Gurion, actually believed Jews were not fully Jewish until they made their home in Israel. In a letter penned some 50 years ago to *Israel Today's* Victor Mordecai, who was growing up in the United States at the time, he wrote: "...If a Jew really wants to be a complete Jew, it is only possible in the Land of Israel... A Jew who wants to be Jewish in everything must come here."

Victor himself wrote in the February 2015 edition of *Israel Today*'s print magazine: "Soon we may see mass Jewish immigration to Israel. Islamic terrorism could be the giant spatula of God to scrape up the Jews and bring them home to Zion." All of which means that Bibi's call could spark what many evangelical Christians believe to be the penultimate fulfilment of prophecy necessary before the end of the age – that is, the re-gathering in the Holy Land of Jews from throughout the diaspora – which will be followed by national recognition of Israel's Messiah.

How appropriate that this rescue call, aimed at ensuring the safety of a people once more in peril, came on the eve of the annual feast of Purim, marking the time when Queen Esther rose up to expose a plot to exterminate her people. 'Je suis Charlie' was seen on many a placard following the terror attack on the *Charlie Hebdo* satirical magazine in Paris, but it was soon adapted to 'Je suis Israel' by those who could see that the ultimate targets were not journalists, but Jews.

I sense the possibility of a divine word puzzle here. 'Je suis' of course means 'I am' in French. Is God, the great 'I AM', assuring us of his presence and everlasting love by saying "I AM Israel"? If you take the 'I' out of 'Je suis' you are left (in English at least) with the name of the One who is recorded as having said: "I am the light of the world..." (John 8.12).

'A greater miracle than the Red Sea crossing'

There are few things clearer in Scripture than the promise of Israel's future restoration. In fact, more than half the prophetic Scriptures relate to the return of the Jewish people to their ancient homeland.[1] John Wesley, perhaps the most revered man of God in English history, wrote: "So many prophecies refer to this grand event that it is surprising any Christian can doubt of it."[2]

The words of the prophet Jeremiah indicate that it would be a greater miracle than the crossing of the Red Sea when some two million Israelites fled Egypt on dry land before the waters closed in on the chasing army: "The days are coming," declares the Lord, "when people will no longer say, 'As surely as the Lord lives, who brought the Israelites up out of Egypt,' but they will say, 'As surely as the Lord lives, who brought the descendants of Israel up out of the land of the north and out of all the countries where he had banished them.' Then they will live in their own land." (Jeremiah 23.7f)

Quoting the Lord again later, he writes: "See, I will bring them from the land of the north and gather them from the ends of the earth." (Jer 31.8) This promise is repeated often (indicating its great importance) by prophets of old, also including Isaiah, Ezekiel, Hosea, Amos, Micah and Zechariah. The Apostle Paul, in his letter to the Roman Christians written specifically to emphasise that God had not turned his back on the Jews because of their apparent rejection of Christ, adds that, when the full number of Gentiles has come in, "all Israel will be saved" (see Romans 11.25f).

It needs to be understood that there are both physical and spiritual applications to many important areas of the Bible's teaching. For example, Jesus said that no-one can see the kingdom of God unless he is born again (see John 3.3-6). So there is physical birth and being born of water and the Spirit.

Israel's restoration is first to the land, and then to the Lord. Notice that the prophecy of Jeremiah 31.8, quoted above, is followed shortly afterwards by God's promise of a new covenant with the house of Israel when he would write his law on their hearts, and they would all "know the Lord" (vv. 31-34). Ezekiel follows the same pattern, first stating that God will bring his people back to their own land (Ezek 36.24) and then, just two verses later, adding that he will give them a new heart and put a new spirit in them!

So, in these latter days, we have witnessed the miracle of Jews returning to their ancient homeland from every corner of the globe in perfect fulfilment of these Scriptures. There are now over six million Jews – nearly half of world Jewry – living in Israel, with ever-increasing numbers of new arrivals, many of whom are fleeing anti-Semitism. At the same time, we are witnessing the unprecedented worldwide growth of so-called Messianic fellowships (of Jews who believe Jesus is their Messiah) along with a rapidly growing openness (even among ultra-Orthodox groups) to the prospect that *Yeshua* (Jesus, in Hebrew) may, after all, be their Messiah. A recent Jews for Jesus survey found that an astonishing 21% (one in five) of Jewish millennials believe Jesus is the Son of God.[3] God has a great future for Israel!

The great re-gathering so far

Aliyah (returning home) began in earnest soon after the re-birth of Israel in 1948 when Operation Magic Carpet brought 47,000 Jews out of Yemen between June 1949 and September 1950. In a secret airlift also known as *Wings of Eagles* and *Messiah's Coming*, British and American transport planes made some 380 flights from Aden in response to an increasingly perilous situation for the Yemenite Jewish community there.

Following the 1947 UN Partition Plan granting a homeland for the Jews, 82 people were killed and a number of Jewish homes destroyed as a result of Muslim riots in Aden. Then, early in 1948, accusations of the murder of two Muslim Yemeni girls led to the looting of Jewish property.

Aden's Jewish community became economically paralysed as most of their stores and businesses were destroyed. And so, in response to an increasingly dangerous situation, the overwhelming majority of Yemenite Jews were secretly airlifted to Israel. Most had never seen an aircraft before – hence the operation's nickname – with many refusing to board out of fear before being reassured when their rabbi reminded them of the biblical origin of its official name – "You yourselves have seen what I did to Egypt, and how I bore you on wings of eagles, and brought you to myself." (Exodus 19.4) And from Isaiah 40.31: "But those who hope in the Lord will renew their strength. They will soar on wings like eagles; they will run and not grow weary, they will walk and not be faint." It was the first in a series of operations whose purpose was to transport entire communities of Jews from Arab countries to Israel *en-masse* during the 1950s and 1960s.

Also in 1950, Operation Ezra and Nehemiah saw a massive 120,000 Jews emigrate to Israel from Iraq, where the Jews were taken during the Babylonian captivity in the sixth century before Christ. Another 75,000 came from North Africa in the period 1948-54. Then, in 1984, *Operation Moses* saw 14,500 Jews airlifted from Ethiopia in just 36 hours, the name reflecting its similarity with the exodus from Egypt led by Moses. Because Jews were forbidden to leave the country, it was again necessary for the operation to remain clandestine.

During the 1990s one million Jews made Aliyah to Israel from the former Soviet Union, many with the help of Christian organisations working with the Jewish Agency, and they also came from Syria, Albania, North and South America, Great Britain, Australia, New Zealand, and a good number (some 80,000) from France, where anti-Semitism is becoming increasingly evident again, especially from the large Muslim community. A total of over three million Jews have returned to the Promised Land since 1948, contributing to nearly half Israel's eight million-plus citizens.

One of the many Christian groups, *Operation Exodus* (a ministry of the Ebenezer Emergency Fund), has helped 130,000 Jews return to Israel over the past 20 years.

More evidence of restoration foretold

Isaiah records that "in that day the Lord will reach out his hand a second time to reclaim the remnant that is left of his people from Assyria, from Lower Egypt, from Upper Egypt, from Cush, from Elam, from Babylonia, from Hamath and from the islands of the sea" (Isa 11.11f), having also just written of a remnant who will "truly rely on the Lord" (Isa 10.20). He later adds: "The Lord will have compassion on Jacob; once again he will choose Israel and will settle them in their own land" (Isa 14.1). He then prophesies about a spiritual highway from Egypt to Assyria via Israel, which will see former enemies worshipping together and blessing one another (Isa 19.23-25). Later he refers to another highway – a Way of Holiness – along which "the ransomed of the Lord will return. They will enter Zion with singing; everlasting joy will crown their heads. Gladness and joy will overtake them, and sorrow and sighing will flee away" (Isa 35.8-10).

Writing of redemption through Israel's only Saviour, he insists: "Do not be afraid, for I am with you; I will bring your children from the east and gather you from the west. I will say to the north, 'Give them up!' and to the south, 'Do not hold them back'" (Isa 43.5f). Then he hints of a time when Gentile evangelists will bring good news (the gospel), as they say to Zion, "Your God reigns!" (Isa 52.7). Their message is summed up in the great prophet's description of what was to happen on the cross of Calvary, just outside the walls of Jerusalem's Old City, where Jesus "was pierced for our transgressions", where, "he was led like a lamb to the slaughter", where, "he bore the sin of many" (See Isa 53).

In terms of the property inheritance of the scattered Jews, there is no doubt, for when they are gathered from the nations, the Sovereign Lord will restore the land of Israel to them. (See Ezek 11.17.) For Ezekiel, the physical and spiritual go hand in hand. The ruins would be rebuilt and the towns resettled, but he would also cleanse them from their sins (Ezek 36.33), adding: "The desolate land will be cultivated instead of lying desolate in the sight of all who pass through it" (v.34). What was known at the time as Palestine was described as a wasteland by 19th century travellers including famous author Mark Twain. But in fulfilment of other prophecies, the desert has since blossomed, producing fruit that has filled the earth.

Ezekiel then writes of a God-given vision of a Valley of Dry Bones in which the Lord announces that he will open the graves of his people and bring them back to the land of Israel. (See Ezek 37.12.) Many, including Israel's Prime Minister Benjamin Netanyahu, believe this scripture was fulfilled when the state of Israel was re-born shortly after the Holocaust that saw six million Jews perish at the merciless hands of the Nazis. The very next two verses state: "Then you, my people, will know that I am the Lord, when I open your graves and bring you up from them. I will put my Spirit in you and you will live, and I will settle you in your own land. Then you will know that I the Lord have spoken, and I have done it, declares the Lord."

The prophet Joel said a time would come when God would make up for all the wasted years in the spiritual wilderness – years of famine, drought and blight. "I will repay you for the years the locusts have eaten" is a promise for those who "rend their heart" and return to the Lord, "who is gracious and compassionate, slow to anger and abounding in love" (Joel 2.13 and 25). The Lord will pour out his Spirit on all people – a prophecy initially fulfilled on the Day of Pentecost but applying also to the very end of the age, when signs and wonders in the heavens would be matched by blood and fire and billows of smoke on the earth. But "everyone who calls on the name of the Lord will be saved; for on Mount Zion and in Jerusalem there will be deliverance..." (Joel 2.28-32).

Amos prophesies of a time when God "will restore David's fallen tent" – "I will repair its broken places, restore its ruins, and build it as it used to be..." (Amos 9.11), and later in the same passage God has further good news: "I will bring back my exiled people Israel; they will rebuild the ruined cities and live in them...I will plant Israel in their own land, never again to be uprooted..." (Amos 9.14f).

Then, in the verse immediately following the well-known prophecy that the Messiah would be born in Bethlehem, Micah adds: "Therefore Israel will be abandoned until the time when she who is in labour gives birth and the rest of his brothers return to join the Israelites" (Micah 5.3). I believe this refers to the subsequent dispersion and re-gathering of the Jews, foretold by our Lord himself. (See Luke 21.24.) Micah, too, speaks of a spiritual restoration: "Do not gloat over me, my enemy! Though I have fallen, I will rise. Though I sit in darkness, the Lord will be my light" (Micah 7.8).

Zephaniah writes of how God will restore their fortunes (in every way) when he gathers them and brings them home. (See Zeph 3.20.) At a time when the nations will be shaken, the Messiah will return and the house of the Lord will be filled with his glory, according to Haggai. (See Haggai 2.6f.) Zechariah speaks for the Almighty when he says: "I will save my people from the countries of the east and the west. I will bring them back to live in Jerusalem; they will be my people, and I will be faithful and righteous to them as their

God... And I will pour out on the house of David and the inhabitants of Jerusalem a spirit of grace and supplication. They will look on me, the one they have pierced, and they will mourn for him as one mourns for an only child, and grieve bitterly for him as one grieves for a firstborn son" (Zech 8.7f, 12.10).

The Apostle Paul, in dealing with God's glorious future plan for the Jews, quotes Isaiah 59.20 thus: "The deliverer will come from Zion; he will turn godlessness away from Jacob." Isaiah continues: "For Zion's sake I will not keep silent... till her righteousness shines out like the dawn, her salvation like a blazing torch" (Isa 62.1). We must pray towards this end, for it is God's perfect will. For those who have been misled into thinking that the Church has somehow replaced Israel in God's affections, hear the word of the Lord to Israel: "I have loved you with an everlasting love... he who appoints the sun to shine by day, who decrees the moon and stars to shine by night, who stirs up the sea so that its waves roar...only if these decrees vanish from my sight will the descendants of Israel ever cease to be a nation before me. Only if the heavens above can be measured and the foundations of the earth below be searched out will I reject all the descendants of Israel because of all they have done" (Jeremiah 31.3, 35-37). On this same theme, he later emphasises: "I will restore their fortunes and have compassion on them" (Jer 33.26). In an apparent reference to the coming thousand-year reign of Christ on earth, Isaiah writes: "They will neither harm nor destroy on all my holy mountain, for the earth will be full of the knowledge of the Lord as the waters cover the sea" (Isa 11.9). The Bible loudly proclaims a glorious future for all God's people, especially his chosen ones.

Some insist that the Jews need to return to the Lord before their restoration to the Land on the basis of a passage in

Deuteronomy that seems to state quite unequivocally that such a re-gathering is dependent on a right relationship with God (Deut 30.1-5). But this does not fit in with the general thread of Scripture on this important teaching. It is clearly outweighed by the plethora of passages pointing to salvation in Israel, along with the precedent set by receiving the Law only after they had been saved from Egypt. That is not to say it is wrong, of course, as "all Scripture is God-breathed" (2 Timothy 3.16). It is just that it needs to be seen in the context of the whole body of Scripture on the subject. Hebraic teacher and author Clifford Denton, more of an expert on these things than I am, says: "I think there has to be an element of 'wait and see' on the fine detail about the way all is fulfilled, however much we cross-reference the scriptures." As with many eschatological details, the Bible sometimes seems deliberately vague or ambiguous. I believe this is so we are not tempted to be too definite on dates, or on the when, where and how of it all. Only God is capable of finishing the jigsaw and sorting out the finer details. Our task is to try to grasp the bigger picture and have a good idea of what to expect and when. The verse immediately preceding this passage, Deuteronomy 29.29, may have a bearing on this issue, i.e. certain matters of eternal significance belong to God alone. Indeed, losing occupation of the land was due to forsaking the law of the Lord. Nevertheless, God would reach out his hand a second time (Isaiah 11.11f). Obviously God teaches his people how to live only after their salvation journey has begun, which is in accordance with the experience of Christians. So the next time the Jews are saved "out of Egypt" (i.e. the nations), they surely would not be required (to be consistent with the rest of Scripture) to know the Lord first. Having said that, many individual Jews – particularly in the U.S. – have come to know Yeshua in their adopted country and subsequently made Aliyah, though many more have yet to leave the comparative comfort of American life.

Notes

[1] *What is God doing in Israel?* by Julia Fisher (Monarch Books) pp 87 & 91

[2] John Wesley's notes on Romans, quoted in *A Nation Called by God* published by Love Never Fails

[3] *Jerusalem Post*, 1 November 2017

POLITICAL DEVELOPMENTS

Chapter 4

Guillotine Wake-Up Call

So how did it all unfold? As we have seen, the revival in understanding of Israel's latter-day restoration goes back centuries. The Puritans, for example, had developed a keen interest in the Jewish people. Indeed, John Wesley came from that background and a man called Andrew Willett had in 1590 written a thesis entirely devoted to the question of the *Calling of the Jews*. Rejecting the Roman Catholic position that the Jews had forfeited the biblical promises by killing Christ, he argued that the term 'Israel' must be taken literally, as referring to the nation and people of Israel, and that, before the return of Christ, the Jewish people would again be established in the land of Israel. The Puritans were dedicated to reform (and a return to biblical practices) from within the church, whereas a somewhat parallel movement, the Separatists, believed such reform was only possible by separating from the established church. The latter group were fiercely persecuted and their leaders became known as the Pilgrim Fathers, who were hounded out of the country in 1608 and subsequently helped to found the United States of America.

The truth about God's eternal love for Israel – for so long hidden in the dark recesses of a church largely unschooled in the scriptures – was now being unveiled as both Puritans and Separatists focused their attention on the light of the Bible. By the time the Wesley brothers came on the scene in the mid-18th century, the people of England were starting to wake up to the reality of the gospel's transforming power.

Both the aristocracy and poorer classes were affected by the revival of biblical Christianity that swept the country. So when John Wesley referred to the coming restoration of Israel, it chimed in perfectly with his biblically-based evangelical messages, for it was firmly founded on the prophecies of the Old Testament.

A severe shock to the national psyche came with the French Revolution of 1789 amid general upheaval in Europe. The British aristocracy were understandably nervous at the prospect of losing their heads if a similar popular uprising occurred on their doorstep, while the professional classes became conscious of the possibility that they were living in the last days, having been made aware of biblical prophecies by the preaching of Wesley, George Whitfield and others. Those who knew their Bible realised they were witnessing signs of the imminent return of Jesus, for which the Jews would need to be back in their ancient homeland, as the scriptures are quite clear on this. It also meant there was an urgent need to preach the gospel to every creature (because the 'end' would come when this was completed – Matthew 24.6-8 and 14) and especially to the Jew (Romans 1.16).

Perhaps a most surprising pioneer of Jewish restoration emerged in the form of the ambitious general and emperor-to-be Napoleon Bonaparte. Some, including Leo Tolstoy in *War and Peace*, had even identified him as the Antichrist, and he did in fact invade the Holy Land in 1798. But in April 1799, while in Galilee, he boldly called upon the exiled Israelites to return to their ancestral home! He published a proclamation inviting "all the Jews of Asia and Africa to gather under his flag in order to re-establish the ancient Jerusalem".[1] He also led the way for the emancipation of Jewish people when he granted liberation to those in a part of Italy then occupied by France who had until then been forced to wear demeaning yellow badges.

Church reaches out to Jews

All of this naturally made British evangelicals even more aware of the urgency of reaching Jewish people for Jesus. So, when thousands of Jewish refugees of the Russian pogroms arrived in London's East End, an obvious door of opportunity had opened. This led to the founding in 1809 of *The London Society for Promoting Christianity among the Jews* (abbreviated to London Jews Society or LJS), an initially non-denominational but later Anglican mission which eventually came to be known as the *Church's Ministry among Jewish people* (CMJ).[2] Slave trade abolitionist William Wilberforce was among the founders and other leading evangelicals such as Charles Simeon were also actively involved. Among the early vice-presidents were the Duke of Devonshire as well as seven earls, five viscounts and several MPs. The Duke of Kent, Queen Victoria's father, became a patron in 1813 and laid the foundation stone of a large complex known as Palestine Place in London's East End. It was an ambitious project amidst the Napoleonic Wars.

Ironically, in view of what I have said about Napoleon, many Jewish refugees came from France, where they had come under persecution along with the protestant Huguenots. The new arrivals were living in poverty and destitution, and Christians duly offered them practical support while at the same time taking heed of the biblical injunction to preach the gospel "first to the Jew, then to the Gentile". More ironically still in view of later developments, it was a German called Joseph Frey who proposed the formalisation of this organisation. Key among the pioneers was Lewis Way, who met Russian Czar Alexander I on three occasions, speaking of the future restoration of the three million Jews within his realm. The Czar was impressed and invited him to address a peace conference where he spoke passionately in front of the leaders of the European nations on behalf of the Jewish people. CMJ duly established centres in Eastern Europe, Russia, the Middle East, Tehran and Morocco, and by the mid-19th century was the biggest missionary organisation in the world, with over 200 missionaries in the field. "The heartbeat of CMJ has always been the sharing of the gospel with Jewish people," former CMJ UK chief Robin Aldridge told me back in 2009, the society's bicentenary, "and we are still very active in Israel."

It was in 1840 that they made the decisive move to establish themselves in Palestine[3] where, on behalf of the British Government, they set up a consulate in Jerusalem – the first European country to do so. They also wanted to build a church but were initially refused permission because the territory was then part of the Turkish Ottoman Empire, where no Christian churches were allowed. But they re-submitted their planning application as a "chapel for the consul and his wife to worship", and Christ Church was duly consecrated in 1849 and is the oldest protestant church in the Middle East.

The consulate was seen as a means of protecting British subjects and travellers among other things – and Foreign Secretary Lord Palmerston finally consented in 1836, following pressure from evangelicals led by his relative Anthony Ashley Cooper (later Lord Shaftesbury), one of the leading social reformers of the time. LJS president Sir Thomas Baring (former Chancellor of the Exchequer) was also involved in the negotiations and William Tanner Young was appointed as consul in 1838. An ecstatic Shaftesbury recorded in his diary: "The ancient city of the people of God is about to resume a place among the nations, and England is the first of Gentile kingdoms that ceases to tread her down." He was referring to the statement by Jesus that "Jerusalem will be trampled on by the Gentiles until the times of the Gentiles are fulfilled" (Luke 21.24b).

Young, also a member of the LJS, was instructed "to

afford protection to the Jews generally" and, in a letter to Palmerston, described the Jew as the one "unto whom God originally gave this land for a possession". Scottish evangelicals also spoke of the blessing of God promised to those who succour his ancient but now afflicted people. During the 1830s and 40s, Lord Shaftesbury petitioned the British Government to support Israel's restoration. As CMJ continued to work both politically and theologically to persuade the government to grant a Jewish homeland in Palestine, they established several centres in the territory while also building hospitals and schools. They built the first school for Jewish children and the first hospitals for their sick and infirm – institutions originally located in Jerusalem's Old City. Owing to their success, however, they soon required bigger premises. The new state-of-the-art buildings designed to meet these increased needs were the first to be constructed outside the city walls.

As a result, they were highly influential in creating an infrastructure for the Jewish state, which also had the effect of provoking the Jews to do even better. For example, after rabbis threatened to excommunicate patients treated at CMJ's hospital, the Jews responded by building their own, Hadassah, now one of the most famous hospitals in the world. Many British evangelicals prayed for and were actively involved in the vision for Jewish restoration. Even the secular press chimed in, with *The Times* declaring: "Let the four Allied Powers now publish to the four quarters of the world their determination to restore the Jews from all nations to the Holy Land, and to assist them in rebuilding the walls and Temple of Jerusalem...." Palmerston certainly took the matter seriously, and made every effort to forward the Jewish cause.

As part of the new diplomatic/spiritual arrangement at Christ Church, meanwhile, a Jew named Michael Solomon

Alexander was appointed the first Protestant Bishop of Jerusalem in a cooperative move with the German church. A Jewish believer in Jesus and a former Rabbi, his consecration in 1841 was the result of a joint LJS/British government proposal – that Britain should work towards a future restoration of the Jewish people to their own land – put forward by Lord Palmerston under the combined influence of his son-in-law Lord Shaftesbury and the Society. In a research paper on the subject, Paul Hames insists that the roots of the Balfour Declaration lay in the appointment of this man, an Anglican minister. For, although the proposal (for Jewish restoration) was shelved at this stage in the face of opposition from the ruling Turks and other international powers, the principle behind it eventually influenced the crucial cabinet meeting of October 1917.

The joint bishopric lasted nearly 50 years, and was the only time the two nations cooperated in protecting and encouraging the Jewish people. But, as pogroms spread across Europe, a Jewish nationalist movement, the *Lovers of Zion*, began agitating for the establishment of a Jewish national home in the land of Israel, and the first wave of immigration came from Russia in the early 1880s.

As already mentioned, the LJS missionaries provided much tangible assistance through the establishment of schools and hospitals, causing the *Jewish Chronicle* correspondent to conclude: "The treatment of these poor Jews is kind in the extreme, and whatever our views as Jews on this subject may be, certain it is that the missionaries have saved many Jewish lives."

Notes

[1] *Anzacs, Empires and Israel's Restoration*, Kelvin Crombie, Vocational Education & Training Publications, p37

[2] Though CMJ was an important forerunner of Christian bodies committed to Israel's restoration, many other groups have since joined the cause and continue to make a powerful contribution both to the defence of Jews and the proclamation of their God. I have included at the end of this book a list of those with which I am familiar.

[3] The name Palestine (or *Palestina*), derived from Israel's ancient enemy the Philistines, was given by the Romans as a final insult following their defeat of the second Jewish Revolt in 135 AD.

Chapter 5

The Pen is Mightier than the Sword!

Theodor Herzl, a Paris-based Austrian journalist, became the inspiration for Zionism in the late 19th century as he awakened worldwide Jewry to his dream of returning to their ancient homeland. After witnessing the rise of anti-Semitism in France, and in particular the shocking mistrial of Captain Alfred Dreyfus, accused of selling military secrets to Germany, he could see the Jews would not be safe anywhere in the diaspora and duly campaigned for the establishment of a Jewish home in Palestine recognised in international law.

In 1896 he outlined his dream in *The Jewish State* and put his case to some of Europe's leaders including Britain's Colonial Secretary Joseph Chamberlain (father of future Prime Minister Neville). He was much encouraged by British clergyman Rev William Hechler who, through his connections with German royalty, set him up for meetings with the Grand Duke of Baden and Kaiser Wilhelm II. Emboldened by these contacts, Herzl tried to persuade the Sultan of Turkey to agree to a Jewish state in Palestine, then under the control of the Turkish Ottoman Empire. Although all these meetings ultimately came to nothing, the Jewish journalist set the ball rolling for the rebirth of Israel with an annual series of International Zion Congresses in Basel, Switzerland, where he was even hailed by some as "King of the Jews" amid scenes of spontaneous singing and dancing, causing an English delegate to express his feelings in an uncharacteristically emotional way, thus: "By the rivers of

Basel we sat down and resolved to weep no more" – adapting the famous lines from Psalm 137.

Herzl declared: "If you will it, it is no dream." But his exhausting efforts put a strain on his health, by his own admission rendering him "old, tired and poor", which led to his untimely death, aged just 44, in 1904, with Rev Hechler beside him in his last days.

Budapest-born Herzl, Paris correspondent for the influential *Neue Freie Presse* in Vienna, initially believed (along with most of the French public) that Dreyfus was guilty, but changed his opinion as he became convinced he had been unfairly prosecuted because he was Jewish. Unable to shake off scenes of the trial, and of the anti-Semitic chants of "Death to the Jews", he spoke of the "slide into barbarism" in France as he became obsessed with finding a solution to the 'Jewish problem'.

Though growing up knowing little of religious Judaism, he became aware of its importance as the movement gained momentum and, for the first time, celebrated Hanukkah instead of Christmas. He committed himself to helping the Jewish people as he became convinced that, by remaining in Europe, they were facing an apocalypse, but got little support from the Jewish aristocracy, about whom he said that "even with all their wealth they were not immune to anti-Semitism" – echoing the message given to Queen Esther by her uncle and guardian Mordecai (Esther 4.13).

On his first trip to London, he was given a standing ovation by the Jewish community leaders and the *Jewish Chronicle* published an excerpt from his book. He was also widely mocked, however, and was even opposed by Orthodox Jews who claimed that "only God in his own time could bring this (restoration to the land) about". According to Alex Jacob in his Olive Press Research Paper *A Synoptic History of Jewish Mission*, Hechler's support was one aspect of a fruitful partnership between political and religious Jewish Zionism and Christian lovers of Zion which had arguably helped Herzl to grow in confidence.

Bizarrely, Herzl's own paper which, even though Jewish-owned was opposed to Zionism, chose not to send a reporter to his congresses, and in fact never even mentioned it. Although when he died they dedicated their entire front page to his obituary, only two sentences spoke of his Zionist activities.

In Britain, as we have seen, there was much sympathy for the Zionist cause, both among politicians and evangelical Christians. But as the Turks appeared unyielding towards negotiations for a Jewish state in Palestine, Chamberlain proposed Uganda as an alternative. Herzl was not interested but later changed his mind in response to anti-Jewish violence in Russia and accepted the offer as a temporary solution. But it did not come to anything.

In accordance with his wishes, his remains were carried to Jerusalem on August 16, 1949 for re-burial at the newly-named Mount Herzl. Naturally, as a journalist myself, I am very proud of his courageous stand for the Jewish people as he swam against the tide of political correctness.

Anglican minister's crucial role

More needs to be said of the crucial role played by the Rev William Hechler. Of German descent, his family moved to England and he followed his father Dietrich into the Anglican ministry. Dietrich actually worked for CMJ and William too became a passionate spokesman for Jewish restoration, declaring: "It is the duty of every Christian to love the Jews." A brilliant man who spoke numerous languages, he became household tutor to the children of Frederick I, Grand Duke of Baden, and through them also got to know the prince who was to become Kaiser Wilhelm II.

He had hoped to be appointed as Bishop of Jerusalem at Christ Church, but deteriorating relations between Prussia and England are said to have blocked this avenue.

It was his appointment as chaplain to the British Embassy in Vienna that was to leave his most lasting legacy, for it was there, in 1896, that he came across Herzl's newly-published book *Der Judenstaadt*, and subsequently made contact with the author. Hechler was also something of a prophet, predicting from meticulous eschatological calculations he had made in 1894 that in 1897 or 1898 a major event would occur that would lead to the restoration of the Jews. He saw, in Herzl's vision, the prophecy fulfilled. Much later, in 1918, Hechler warned the Jewish world that a terrible calamity of horrific dimensions was coming if the Jews did not return to Palestine.

Meanwhile the Grand Duke became a lifelong advocate of Herzl, using his office and relationship with his nephew, the Kaiser, to support the Zionist cause. The Kaiser's 1898 trip to Jerusalem – to visit German settlements and rededicate Christ Church (focus of the Anglo-German bishopric) – provided "immense impetus" for the cause of Zionism, according to the London *Daily Mail*,[1] Britain's most popular newspaper of the time. This was indeed the perception, but in fact the Kaiser had by now backed away from supporting Herzl. Nevertheless, in the eyes of the world's press, Hechler had succeeded in bringing political legitimacy to Zionism.

The somewhat eccentric clergyman, who was also a founding member of the First Vienna Football Club, was to attend five Zionist Congresses as Herzl's aide and friend, and was at his side the day before he died – the last non-family member to be with him. Herzl's last words to him were: "Greet Palestine for me. I gave my heart's blood for my people."

Before his death, Herzl had asked that the Zionist

community remember and honour Hechler for all he had done for him and Zionism. Beginning in the late 1920s, the Zionist Executive provided him with a £10 monthly pension. He died in 1931 at Mildmay Hospital[2] where he had worked until shortly before his death while living in Highgate, north London. He was buried in an unmarked grave in New Southgate Cemetery, a few miles away, but the site has since been rediscovered and, led by the Jewish American Society for Historic Preservation and the British Christian Zionist Movement, an appropriate memorial was erected there on January 31, 2011.

The Jewish community of Vienna had proposed in 1934 that a statue be erected in his honour, but this was never done. His predictions of a coming catastrophe were tragically fulfilled soon afterwards. Though Hechler had failed in his efforts to get full German recognition of Zionism, world power endorsement would come from his mother's homeland (Britain) rather than his father's.

Another partnership between Jew and Gentile was key to the furtherance of the dream of a revived Jewish homeland. Chaim Weizmann, one of 15 children born to a Jewish couple in Belarus, studied biochemistry in Germany and moved to Manchester in 1904, aged 30, becoming a leading figure of Britain's Zionist movement in the years that followed, as well as a top biochemist. During World War I he developed an important chemical ingredient for gunpowder, which brought him to the attention of the British Government and, in particular, Lord Balfour, with whom he had already become friends.

Scottish-born Arthur Balfour became MP for Manchester East (where he first met Weizmann) in 1885 and was Prime Minister from 1902-5. At the time of the Balfour Declaration in 1917, he was Foreign Secretary. Weizmann managed to persuade Balfour, an evangelical Christian, of the case for a homeland for the Jewish people in what was then known as 'Palestine'.

Britain's strategic needs, burgeoning alliances with Arab leaders and the clear justice of the Zionists' dreams coalesced on 31 October, 1917 when the War Cabinet (most of whom were also evangelical Christians) agreed the final wording of a letter to Lord Rothschild and the Zionist Federation – a letter which became known as the Balfour Declaration since Balfour was the signatory.[3]

Notes

[1] *Daily Mail*, 18 November 1898

[2] A Christian mission hospital originally set up to cater for the medical needs of slum-dwellers in London's East End, and now specializing in the treatment of HIV patients.

[3] With thanks to Elim minister Rev Nick Gray for his insights on Chaim Weizmann (*Heart Publications*, February-March 2017)

All the material on Herzl is taken from *It is no dream – the life of Theodor Herzl*, from the Moriah Films Collection of the Simon Wiesenthal Centre. Much of the information on Rev Hechler has been gleaned, with thanks, from Wikipedia – though I am also indebted, as indicated in the text, to the insights of Rev Alex Jacob.

Chapter 6

Battle for Jerusalem

Some 85,000 Jewish people lived in Turkish Palestine at the outbreak of World War I in 1914. A number were attacked and deported to Egypt where, by March 1915, there were some 10,000 Jewish refugees. However, many of them contributed to the war effort as members of the Zion Mule Corps (later the Jewish Legion) under the command of Anglo-Irish evangelical John Patterson who had a deep love for the Jewish people and was a firm believer in their restoration.

The Gallipoli venture of 1915 – the attempt to control the Dardanelles Straits – had been seen as a military disaster resulting in the death of some 8,000 Australian and New Zealand soldiers (known as ANZACS). But, with the benefit of hindsight, it was to prove a useful diversion of the war from an Allied perspective. And the Anzacs were to play a crucial role in the liberation of the Holy Land towards the end of 1917, particularly through the Battle of Beersheva, a key town in the Negev desert some 50 miles south-west of Jerusalem.

The man in charge, General Edmund Allenby, is said to have carried with him a message from Prime Minister Lloyd George, who "wanted Jerusalem as a Christmas present for the British nation". Meanwhile, Lord Arthur Balfour, the Foreign Secretary, was in touch with Lord Walter Rothschild, representing the Zionist movement, over the prospect of Jewish restoration. Balfour was, however, under pressure to postpone the issue, but insisted "this was a question on which the Foreign Office had been very strongly pressed for a long time past". Nevertheless, fearing a backlash against the Jews, the British Government regarded as essential that any public announcement of sympathy towards Zionism be coupled with a military breakthrough.

Soldiers from Down Under come up trumps for Israel

So it was that, at 4.30pm on October 31, 1917, about 800 bayonet-wielding Australian horsemen set off in three columns at a canter across a 5 km plain to Beersheva on an epic cavalry charge that, in Australian author Kelvin Crombie's words, would change the course of world history. They were evidently riding a gauntlet of shrapnel, high explosives and machine-gun fire, and their rapid advance prevented the intended complete destruction of local wells, which would have been disastrous for over 50,000 soldiers and their animals.

Though Britain undoubtedly played a major role in Israel's restoration, it is only fair to record for posterity the vital contribution made by our Antipodean friends from Down Under. For the outcome for which so many had sought and prayed over centuries became a practical possibility within weeks when General Allenby's forces took Jerusalem from the Turks, but without the brave ANZAC forces this could surely not have happened. The Jewish people remain forever in their debt.

Against all odds, the legendary charge of the ANZAC light horse brigade completed a victory in the Battle of Beersheva that might not otherwise have been possible, and paved the way for the subsequent capture of Jerusalem, bringing the centuries-old Ottoman Empire to an ignominious end in the process. ANZAC Day is now held each year on April 25th to mark the landing on Turkey's Gallipoli Peninsula in 1915 of Australian and New Zealand forces, who subsequently conducted a brave eight-month long campaign against fierce opposition, and is a day of remembrance for all 60,000 ANZACs who fell during World War I.

So it was that, on the very day that the British Government promised to do all in its power to establish a Jewish national home in what was then known as Palestine (October 31, 1917), British and ANZAC troops captured Beersheva, the first military victory in the campaign to liberate the land of Israel from the Turks. Jerusalem was duly captured on December 9. It would appear that for some reason only known to God, he used people from the farthest ends of the earth in a very pivotal way to establish his purposes for Israel. It is perhaps because of this important link more than any current involvement with fighting terrorism in the region that Islamic State apparently sought to mark a recent ANZAC Day with an attack in Melbourne, which was thankfully foiled.

There is more. At Rosh Ha Nikra, on the border with Lebanon, there is a plaque commemorating the role of New Zealanders in building the railway line which was supposed to extend from Egypt to Turkey. Unfortunately, it had to be bombed during World War II to prevent the enemy using it for troop transportation.

Close to the border with Gaza, there is a special memorial to the New Zealand soldiers who fought in the Holy Land in both world wars. It is perfectly fitting, therefore, that Aussies and Kiwis (especially the Christians among them) continue to play a key role in various efforts to bless and support Israel today.

But the Anzacs were not the only heroes of the hour. Cpl John Collins of the Welsh Fusiliers won the VC for his brave actions during this battle. Welsh heroism became legendary following the award of eleven VCs for the Battle of Rorke's Drift during the Zulu War of 1879 – the most ever awarded in a single engagement and famously championed in the iconic movie *Zulu*, starring Michael Caine. I grew up close to the site and watched some of the episodes being filmed.

On the very day when British newspapers reported the victory at Beersheva (2 November, 1917), Balfour conveyed the Cabinet's decision (on Jewish restoration) to Rothschild:

> His Majesty's Government views with favour the establishment in Palestine of a national home for the Jewish people, and will use its best endeavours to facilitate the achievement of this object, it being clearly understood that nothing shall be done which may prejudice the civil and religious rights of existing non-Jewish communities in Palestine, or the rights and political status enjoyed by Jews in any other country.

It all climaxed at a town connected to Abraham, the father of Israel to whom, the Bible states, God had promised the land as an eternal possession.

The Royal Flying Corps played a vital role in the subsequent capture of Jerusalem by surveying Turko-German troop movements and dropping countless pamphlets calling upon the Turks to surrender, an event evidently foretold by Isaiah some 2,600 years earlier when he wrote: "Like birds hovering overhead, the Lord Almighty will shield Jerusalem; he will shield it and deliver it, he will 'pass over' it and will rescue it" (Isa 31.5). As it happens, this passage was also the required reading in all Anglican churches in Britain that week. As a result, Jerusalem surrendered without a shot being fired, apparently because the leaflets were signed *Allenby,* understood by the Arabic-reading population to be *Al-Nebbi*, i.e. *The Prophet* (Mohammed). Victory in Jerusalem marked the end of 400 years of Turkish Muslim rule and coincided with the Hanukkah festival recalling Jewish liberation from

Greek-Syrian tyranny in the second century before Christ, giving double reason for celebrations. One Aussie trooper is reported to have fallen off his horse following too much wine sampling from grateful residents.

The eight-day festival of Hanukkah is an especially joyous time for Jews and marks God's intervention at the time of the reign of the ruthless emperor Antiochus Epiphanes, who desecrated the Jewish Temple by sacrificing a pig there and blasphemously proclaimed himself god. Judah Maccabee led a brave and successful revolt against the tyrant in 164 BC and re-established Temple worship ('Hanukkah' means *dedication*) with the aid of the menorah (seven-branched candlestick) which burned miraculously for eight days despite having only enough oil for a day. The Greeks had polluted the rest. Not surprisingly, public places are suitably festooned with colourful lights, rather as Christians celebrate the approach of Christmas. In fact, the two festivals come close together, and I believe this is rather apt. In my opinion the feast also foreshadows the coming of the Jewish Messiah *Yeshua*, who described himself as "the light of the world" (John 8.12) and whom many believe was conceived at Hanukkah and born during the Feast of Tabernacles.

Allenby's official entry came on December 11 when, after meeting with other military chiefs at temporary headquarters established at the CMJ hospital (now the Anglican International School, still under CMJ) on Prophets Street, he proceeded on horseback to the Old City (about one kilometre away), dismounting at Jaffa Gate and entering the holy enclave on foot, declaring: "It does not behove me, a Christian, to enter the City of my Messiah mounted." He was met by a guard of honour of British and Anzac[1] soldiers, and declared British military rule from the ancient steps of the Tower of David, right opposite Christ Church, the CMJ headquarters.

Apparently, all the photographs of that historic occasion were taken from on top of the buildings of the Christ Church compound. One photograph has become very familiar to me, having visited three times in recent years. The scene is virtually unchanged, except that the soldiers are largely replaced by crowds of tourists and pilgrims. Among the party accompanying Allenby was Col T E Lawrence (of Arabia fame). A New Zealand soldier, Louis Salek, daringly ascended the tower to hoist the Jewish flag atop the very building reputedly left standing by the Romans in 70 AD (there is some doubt as to whether it is the original tower), presumably to signal the official restoration of Jewish national life in the land after 1,800 years. The LJS response to these events quoted Jesus' prophecy in Luke 21.24 that "Jerusalem shall be trodden down of the Gentiles until the times of the Gentiles be fulfilled". After the ceremony, Crombie reports in his book *Restoring Israel*,[2] Allenby and his entourage returned to General Shea's headquarters at the CMJ hospital for lunch, adding: "It was only fitting that both of CMJ's Jerusalem properties were involved on that historic and auspicious occasion."

Though of course the military played a significant role in Jewish restoration, it was essentially a spiritual movement. Looking back on these momentous times, English Jewish historian Leonard Stein, in his 1961 book *The Balfour Declaration* (London), wrote that, "The real force behind the movement for the restoration of the Jews to Palestine was the 'religious party' ...a body of devout and high-minded English Christians who, looking at the ferment in the East, believed that the time was at hand for the fulfilment of prophecy by the return of the Chosen People to the Holy Land, and that it was God's will that the British nation should be the instrument of achieving this purpose".

The Magnificent Ten

Believing that Christian Zionism was at the heart of the British Government's decision to declare its support for Jewish repatriation to their ancient land, Jerusalem-based Canadian academic Dr David Schmidt shared his research into the ten members of British Prime Minister David Lloyd George's 1917 War Cabinet with a significant body of church leaders at London's City Temple in January 2017.[3] Though from different social backgrounds and representing all contemporary political parties, these magnificent ten were, for the most part, nonconformist evangelical Christians – there were no Anglicans – who were familiar with the Old Testament and aware of biblical prophecy. Ironically, the only Jewish member strongly opposed the policy. Many Jews at the time saw it as being herded into a 'ghetto'. But their opposition gradually faded as the Zionist movement gained momentum.

Lloyd George was the main figure behind the declaration, said Dr Schmidt. Though "ethically challenged" – he had a mistress, for one thing – the Welsh-born Liberal Prime Minister was raised on the Bible and retained a sentimental attachment to biblical values while not always living up to its high ideals.

Balfour, too, was steeped in the Bible from his Scottish Presbyterian childhood, believing that Christian civilisation owed an immeasurable debt to Judaism. He was motivated by what he called "the desire to give the Jews their rightful place in the world" and even gave theological lectures at Cambridge University. He was highly accomplished, having already served as Prime Minister, and declared on his deathbed that aiding Jewish restoration was possibly the most worthwhile thing he had done. He asked that the inscription on his tombstone should read, "I have fought the good fight, I have finished the race, I have kept the faith," quoting the apostle Paul in 2 Timothy 4.7.

Also in the cabinet was Jan Christiaan Smuts, a Boer general in the South African War. Raised in the Reform Church, his early life was filled with Bible teaching and he predicted that, in generations to come, a great Jewish state would arise once more. In fact, Smuts argued for the biblical restoration of Israel all his life. He was the only Cabinet member who lived to see the reborn state when, as South African Prime Minister, he was the first to recognise the new country after the United States.

Edward Carson, a fiery criminal lawyer from Ulster, opposed Lloyd George on many other issues, but not this one.

Andrew Bonar Law, a Canadian raised by a Presbyterian minister, became Prime Minister in 1922, but died of cancer soon afterwards.

Labour politician Arthur Henderson was converted to Christ through the famed evangelist Gypsy Smith and was also a wholehearted supporter of the Balfour Declaration, as was fellow Labour member George Barnes, who loved the Jewish people.

Support also came from Alfred Milner (brought up in Germany) but George Nathaniel Curzon raised early objections. As a former Viceroy of India, he understood how the Muslims could rise up in opposition and believed the Jews would struggle to live in such "a desolate place".

Edwin Montague, meanwhile, was opposed both to the declaration and to Zionism in general despite being a Jew himself because it would force a nationality on people who had nothing in common, and become a Jewish ghetto.

Notes

[1] It would appear that the Australians endeared themselves to the Jews for their friendliness and generosity.

[2] An account of CMJ's first 200 years published in 2008 by Nicolayson's Ltd at Christ Church.

[3] Dr David Schmidt's London lecture at the City Temple, Holborn, on January 25 2017. For his full research into the subject, see his book *Partners Together in this Great Enterprise – The Role of Christian Zionism in the Foreign Policies of Britain and America in the 20th Century,* published by Xulon Press and available from Amazon.

I am also indebted for some historical facts in this chapter to Dov Chaikin of *Israel Today*.

Chapter 7

Storm Clouds Gather

But the political passage to full restoration was about to enter stormy seas, and it was a miracle that the whole enterprise wasn't shipwrecked on the rocks of betrayal and anti-Semitism. The Balfour Declaration, through which the British Government had promised to do all in its power to establish a homeland for the Jews, was only weeks old when the opportunity to fulfil that pledge was evidently handed on a plate – with Jerusalem in British hands. But it was not to be that simple as it seemed that all the hordes of hell were determined to stop Jewish immigration. The Holy Land had become a sparsely populated, uncared for, barren wasteland, in fulfilment of Scripture. But now that there was a serious intention among the nations to approve of a Jewish return, the Arab nations of the Middle East strongly objected, and it seemed no-one was prepared to upset them.

Unfortunately, many of the British officials and officers in Palestine refused to accept the Balfour Declaration, and hardly endeared themselves to those in their care when in April 1919 Jewish soldiers were not permitted to celebrate Passover in Jerusalem. But it was not only the Jews who felt the short end of the stick from the British. When a New Zealand soldier was shot dead as he gave chase to a thief who had stolen into his tent, his incensed colleagues believed nothing was done by the authorities to bring the culpable Arab to account, and this became a constant theme of life in the region over the years that followed. In July a

British general publicly maligned the Jewish Legion who had fought in the war on our behalf, and even struck a soldier with his cane. Adding insult to injury, Vladimir Jabotinski (a leading Jewish officer) was summarily drummed out of the British Army.

A group of local Arabs then presented the British authorities with a resolution opposing Zionism, and petitioning that 'Palestine' become part of Greater Syria. Subsequent attacks on Jewish settlements coincided with an increase in anti-Zionism within the British administration, which in turn led to the formation of Haganah, a Jewish self-defence group. Yet despite all this opposition, which had the effect of steering the restoration process somewhat off course, the international peace treaties that followed the war paved the way for modern Israel. Britain's Mandate (responsibility) for Palestine was officially confirmed at the San Remo conference on the Italian Riviera in 1920 and unanimously agreed in 1922 by the 51 members of the Council of League of Nations, the latter body having been formed to keep the peace and redraw international boundaries. Britain was thus charged with being "solely responsible for placing the country under such political, administrative and economic conditions as will secure the establishment of the Jewish national home."

At the same time a large Arab mob, partly led by Haj Amin al-Husseini who had been appointed the Mufti (Muslim spiritual leader) of Jerusalem in 1921 (later claiming the title Grand Mufti), began to attack Jewish people in the Old City and continued their pogrom into the Jewish Quarter, killing six Jews and wounding some 200. But the Haganah were barred from entry by British troops and Jabotinsky was sentenced to 15 years' imprisonment at a closed Court Martial after becoming a suitable scapegoat for the mayhem. This sparked an outcry in the British Parliament and the

Government finally realised that the military administration was not fulfilling its pro-Zionist policies. Lloyd George replaced the military administration with a civil one, and Herbert Samuel became the first High Commissioner.

All this more or less coincided with the decision at San Remo to confer a Mandate upon Britain for the land of Israel, thus entrusting her with responsibility for fulfilling the Balfour Declaration. But the British Mandate came under increasing pressure as anti-Zionist propaganda spread. With the stroke of a pen, Winston Churchill detached Transjordan from the rest of Palestine and declared that no Jewish settlement was permitted there. Not surprisingly, the Zionist movement were disappointed that some 75% of the land promised in the Balfour Declaration was now made off-limits to the Jewish people. Yet the Arab nationalists, represented by al-Husseini, rejected the compromise solution out of hand – they wanted all Balfour's promises declared null and void. In May, 18 young Jewish immigrants were killed by a bomb in Jaffa, and a pogrom subsequently spread out from there.

Opposition to the mandate mounted in Britain, but fortunately Churchill (as Colonial Secretary) persuaded them to honour their wartime pledges. As the restoration of the Jewish homeland progressed, many Arabs from neighbouring lands entered British Palestine, enjoying the economic benefits by now in evidence. However, pogroms erupted in 1929 after young Jews demonstrated allegiance to their holy place at the Western Wall. Jewish communities throughout the land were savagely attacked, and in Hebron 66 innocent Jews were massacred.

Lydia's baptism of fire

Among the eye-witnesses of these frightening disturbances was a remarkable young woman from Denmark who had an encounter with Christ and went on to fulfil her destiny in a city she knew nothing about, allowing the Holy Spirit to guide her every step. Much later, with the help of her husband Derek Prince, she would commit her extraordinary story to print with the publication of *Appointment in Jerusalem.*

Lydia Christensen was a schoolteacher in her mid-thirties, living very comfortably as her local school's head of domestic science. But she was searching for God, whom she could not find in her Lutheran surroundings. She even turned down a marriage proposal for fear it would detract from her determined quest to discover whether Jesus was real. When He appeared to her in a vision, her miraculous journey of faith had begun.

Other visions followed, she began to speak in a language she had never learnt, and was soon baptised in the sea by a Pentecostal pastor, sparking much ridicule and scorn from her colleagues and pupils. It was through a vision of people in Middle Eastern dress that she felt a call to Jerusalem. She gave away her possessions and set off, in 1928, for the 'City of the Great King', as the psalmist describes it (Psalm 48.2). Like Abraham, she did not know where she was going to stay or how she was going to make ends meet, especially as she had no work permit. She only knew God had called her there. At one point she was down to her last 86 cents and went without food for four days, but it only deepened her trust.

Her first task came as quite a shock. A Jewish man, having heard that she was a kind woman, came to ask her if she would look after his dying baby daughter. Initially protesting her inexperience, she took her in and anointed her with oil as she prayed for her healing in Jesus' name. Tikva (meaning 'hope' in Hebrew) made a remarkable recovery, so much so that her parents wanted her back, by which time Lydia had grown to love her as her own. But she realised she had to offer her up as a sacrifice, as Abraham had done with Isaac and, just as in the biblical narrative, she did receive Tikva back because it turned out her parents were unable to cope.

When serious riots broke out between Jews and Arabs in 1929, she was forced to run the gauntlet of no-go areas in order to fetch water, which had been cut off by the fighting. When she struggled to get over the barricades with Tikva on her shoulders, suddenly – out of nowhere – a man came to her rescue. When she told her friends what had happened, they were all convinced it must have been an angel!

Others were leaving the city because of the tension, but Lydia believed God was calling her to be a "watchman on the walls" (Isaiah 62.6), praying for the peace of Jerusalem. In the ensuing years she continued to mother scores of abandoned Jewish and Arab children. She also realised the city held the key to the world's future and that Christians need to do all they can to help Israel. "We owe them a huge debt which has gone unpaid for too many centuries," she wrote to her mother. "It is to them that we owe the Bible, the prophets, the apostles, the Saviour Himself."

Perhaps if such calls had been heeded on a wider basis, millions of Jews could have been saved from the Holocaust which was to come. At the end of World War II, Lydia married Derek Prince, the well-known Bible teacher, and *Appointment in Jerusalem* was published by Kingsway in 1975.

The Charismatic movement,[1] of which Lydia was clearly a pioneer, was in its early stages then, and in fact flourishing. But it has lost its momentum, its certainty, its confidence. Tragically, the Western church has lost its focus on the gospel, along with the Holy Spirit whose empowering we need to proclaim it. We have also taken our eye off God's end-time purposes for Israel and the world.

A group of evangelical preachers, in their so-called Berlin Declaration of 1909, decided that the Pentecostal outpouring at Azusa Street in Los Angeles (1906) and Sunderland, England (1907) was not of God. I am afraid this amounted to blasphemy of the Holy Spirit and paved the way for the Holocaust. Some churches need to do a lot of repenting. They neither have the Spirit nor any understanding of what is happening in today's world – when all the while the Bible is there to tell us! The prophecies of Scripture should light up our paths in a dark and oppressive world (see 2 Peter 1.19-21). We ought to know the meaning of all the chaos, anarchy, bloodshed and terror raging across Europe and the Middle East. We ought to be able to instruct others and warn them of the judgment to come. As Derek Prince wrote: "For the unbeliever, the world around is getting darker.... For the believer, however, the light of prophetic revelation, like a lamp, shines more brightly by contrast with the surrounding darkness."

When you are led by the Spirit as you study the Word (bearing in mind that the Spirit leads us into all truth – see John 16.13), you will understand the signs of the times, especially as they relate to Israel, God's chosen. There is a consistent and indelible link between Holy Spirit revival and the cause of Zionism, by which I mean the restoration of Jews to their Land and their God. The Pentecostal outpouring to which I have referred followed closely on the heels of the beginnings of Zionism under Theodor Herzl, while the Spirit-led influence of the Wesleys, Wilberforce, Simeon, Spurgeon and Bishop J C Ryle had all helped create political sympathy for a Jewish homeland.

I am encouraged, however, that amidst our backsliding, some movements (such as the Keswick Convention) are working towards a converging of the Spirit and the Word, a notion that would have gladdened the heart of Pentecostal pioneer Donald Gee. I add a testimony from sixty years ago, when R T Kendall (who graced the pulpit of Westminster Chapel for 25 years) had his own Damascus Road experience,[2] which he said preserved him from liberalism.[3]

Many of his colleagues from his days with the once-influential Nazarene denomination no longer believe in the infallibility of the Bible. "Some orthodox people poke fun at the idea that 'a man with an experience is never at the mercy of a man with an argument'. Cold, dead orthodoxy often depends on argument or reason to support Scripture. But I have *both* – thanks to the Holy Spirit unveiling truth in the Word of God. I can defend what I believe; I would go to the stake for what I believe. This is why we need the Word and the Spirit together."[4]

Thankfully, CMJ was birthed during the great evangelical awakening which opened eyes to a right understanding of God's purposes for the Jews. I agree with CMJ's former UK chief Robin Aldridge, who believes that when the Church experiences a deeper dimension of the Holy Spirit, it is generally accompanied by a greater understanding of Israel. After all, Jesus said the Spirit would lead us into all truth!

The general who stopped the war!

Thankfully, the 1929 riots were put down with the help of the same British officer who effectively stopped World War I. Like Patterson, General William Dobbie was a Bible-believing Christian who resorted to prayer in seeking the wisdom needed to stop the attacks. He had actually given the order to lay down arms in 1918 and was recently the subject of a year-long exhibition at Jerusalem's Christ Church,[5] which has strong links to his family.

When the riots broke out as Arabs became anxious about growing Jewish immigration, the then Brigadier Dobbie – a distant cousin of T E Lawrence – successfully brought calm to the situation as he sought God's guidance! With very few troops and widespread disorder throughout the country, the career army officer and devout Christian was faced with a dilemma. Rejecting outright such suggestions as placing the country under martial law or requesting RAF bombing raids on Arab villages, Dobbie turned to prayer. It was hardly a textbook tactic but, when reinforcements arrived, he spread his men very thinly to cover as wide an area as possible, and the violence ceased in the early stages before things got out of hand. Out of gratitude, the Jewish community of Hebron presented Dobbie with a silver Hebrew Bible.

As the staff officer on duty on November 11, 1918, Dobbie (then a Lt Colonel) signed the telegram calling for hostilities to cease at 1100 hours. He actually fought on the front line in all three major wars of the 20th century, starting with the Anglo-Boer War of 1899-1902. In April 1940 he came out of retirement and helped turn the tide of World War II as he led the defence of Malta, the most bombed place on earth. The general's son, Colonel Orde Dobbie, was a member of Christ Church with his wife Flo while living in Jerusalem during the 1970s and 80s, during which time he led a future British General, Tim Cross, to faith in Christ while on an Easter visit to Israel. His grandson, Jos Johnston, helped to set up the exhibition.

In the foreword to his memoirs – *A Very Present Help* – Gen Dobbie wrote:

> During the course of a long, varied and interesting military career I have had many tokens of God's great goodness to me. I have seen his overruling control in my life and his guidance in my affairs... I desire to emphasize, especially to the rising generation, that it is a practical and intensely real thing to let Christ come into one's life, and that today,

as ever before, it is no vain thing to trust in the living God."

It was while commanding troops in the Holy Land in 1929 that he gave New Testaments to his soldiers, with the following inscription:

> You are stationed at the place where the central event in human history occurred – namely the crucifixion and death of the Son of God. You may see where this took place and you may read the details in this Book. As you do so, you cannot help being interested, but your interest will change into something far deeper when you realize that that event concerns you personally and that it was for your sake that the Son of God died on the cross here. The realization of this fact cannot but produce a radical change in one's life – and the study of this book will, under God's guidance, help you to such a realization.

Notes

[1] A Holy Spirit outpouring among the old, established churches.
[2] Jesus appeared to him in a vision as he was driving his car.
[3] A liberal interpretation of the Scriptures; non-acceptance of its ultimate authority.
[4] Article by R T Kendall published in Premier Christian Radio online magazine November 2015.
[5] Appropriately enough, in view of Gen Dobbie's achievement in restoring calm to Arab-Jewish conflict, Christ Church continues to reach out to both Jew and Arab with the message of Jesus as the long-awaited Messiah.

Chapter 8

The Sky Darkens

To be sure, the intervention of Dobbie's forces obviously helped save the lives of many stricken Jewish and European people. Ramsay MacDonald's Shaw Commission subsequently concluded that the riots were a natural reaction of the Arab population against Zionism and the Balfour Declaration. A 1930 White Paper called for limitations upon Jewish immigration and settlement – the first official attempt by the British Government to break the commitment she had given to the Jewish people, as endorsed by the League of Nations Mandate. Fortunately, its harsh proposals were later virtually cancelled following strong opposition.

Following 1930, as the number of German Jewish refugees increased, so too did local Arab opposition – and more riots broke out. In response to further Arab pressure, Britain limited the quota of Jewish entry visas in 1934. Further riots in 1936 led to sabotage and terrorism, primarily against the Jewish community. Seemingly incapable of protecting Jewish lives, Britain was forced to 'legalise' a special police force. Ominously, swastikas began appearing in Jerusalem.

The so-called Peel Commission subsequently proposed partitioning the now already severely reduced land allocation for Israel into two states – one Jewish and the other Arab (the latter linked to Transjordan). But radical Arabs insisted on no Jewish state at all and al-Husseini ignited an intimidation campaign which led to the murder of Lewis Andrews, the British Governor of the Galilee district, in September 1937. Al-Husseini took sanctuary on the Temple Mount and from there, under disguise, escaped to Lebanon. A revolt followed, leading to yet more sabotage and death.

As Hitler's troops took over Austria in March 1938, thousands more Jews sought refuge from Nazi persecution. Western democracies held a conference on their plight at the French resort of Evian, but stopped short of offering any tangible assistance. Colonel Orde Charles Wingate, nephew of General Dobbie, was duly dispatched to take charge of a Jewish police force. He was also Zionist in persuasion and carried a Bible with him at all times. But when Jews were forced to flee Czechoslovakia following Hitler's invasion in 1939, only a few were permitted entry to the Holy Land. Others entered illegally, alongside many Polish and German Jews. Colonial Secretary Malcolm MacDonald then all but rescinded the Balfour promises in a White Paper – there would be no specific Jewish State, instead of which there would be a State of Palestine with an Arab majority. In addition, Jewish immigration was limited to some 75,000 people over the next five years, and Jewish purchase of land and property was virtually outlawed. The League of Nations Mandates Commission responded by accusing Britain of a flagrant breach of its Mandate. At a time when millions of immigration certificates were needed, Britain failed to honour even this commitment, refusing entry to many who were trying to flee Nazi-occupied Europe and deporting them to places like Mauritius. At the end of the war 36,000 immigration certificates remained unused!

The declaration of war launched a reign of terror on Poland's three million Jews. The Nazi machine made no secret of its sympathy with nationalist Arab ambitions of completely eradicating the Jewish presence in Palestine where fear of an Arab uprising gripped the British authorities, causing them to place severe restrictions on Jewish immigration, and come down heavily on the Haganah, putting 43 of their men on trial. In 1941 pro-Mufti groups ransacked the Jewish quarter of Baghdad and massacred 180 innocent Jewish civilians, an atrocity which stood as ample evidence of the brutality and intentions of the pro-Axis Arab nationalist movement and its unofficial leader al-Husseini. It certainly highlighted the need to keep any Axis-Arab force from taking control over areas where Jewish people lived, most notably in Israel. Quite understandably, Jews in Palestine were deeply concerned about German presence in Syria (Anzacs were instrumental in eventually subduing the region), and Jewish newspapers carried almost daily reports of the deteriorating conditions for their European communities under Nazi control.

Meanwhile al-Husseini, on Berlin Radio, called on the Moslems of the world to join the Axis in a Jihad (Holy War) against the Allies. On January 20, 1942 Gestapo chief Reinhard Heydrich produced a document outlining the plan for the systematic destruction of the entire Jewish population of Europe – the so-called 'Final Solution' for Europe's eleven million Jews. Everyone knew the terrible consequences if the Germans invaded the land of Israel, threatening its 550,000 Jews with annihilation. Clearly, Jewish survival in the land was reliant on an Allied victory in the region, to which Jews significantly contributed.

Although Churchill was working behind the scenes on Israel's behalf, the fact remained that the Jewish people of Europe were being exterminated, and the Land of Israel was now closed to those who could flee. Jewish patience was running out and, on 1 January, 1944, the Irgun, an offshoot of Haganah, declared armed revolt against the British authorities. This paramilitary organisation came under the command of future Prime Minister Menachem Begin, who had fled Nazi-occupied Poland in 1943.

The opening session of the newly-formed United Nations

was held in San Francisco in April 1945, the qualification for entrance being participation in the war against the Axis forces. In the end four Arab nations were accepted, including Egypt, Yemen and Saudi Arabia, who were encouraged by Britain to quickly declare war against Germany so as to qualify. Yet most of the leaders of the Arab countries had actually supported the German cause during the war!

A committee proposed by new Foreign Secretary Ernest Bevin called for the immediate entry of 100,000 war refugees into British Palestine. But within days, a friendship treaty was signed by newly-independent Transjordan's King Abdullah, and the door was abruptly closed on the refugees. The pro-Allied role of Palestine's Jews was being forgotten, as was the pro-Nazi position of many of the Arab leaders. As Irgun activities intensified, the British authorities evacuated all dependents to Britain in February 1947 and subsequently hanged four Jewish freedom fighters at Acre Prison. A particularly shocking episode involved a dilapidated old ship, the *Exodus*, carrying 4,554 Jewish refugees, which got caught up in a running battle with the Royal Navy, leaving three dead and scores wounded. The ship was turned back from Haifa, and the refugees were returned first to France and then, unbelievably, back to Germany, where their compatriots had just been slaughtered in their millions. It seemed the British authorities were determined to hinder every effort of the Jewish people to reach their ancient homeland.

Ironically, the UN was at the same time finalising a report calling for an end to the British Mandate, and recommending the establishment of a Jewish State, an Arab State, and the internationalisation of Jerusalem. But it was rejected outright by the Arabs, which in turn alarmed the 700,000 Jews living within the Arab countries. Arab oil was of course also a factor by now.

Finally, on November 29 1947, the UN voted to recognise Israel with the required two-thirds majority. I am glad to say that Australia, New Zealand, South Africa and the United States, where the rest of my family live, were among those who supported Zionism. Britain, I am ashamed to say (and I have strong roots here too), abstained. Yet amidst further terror being rained upon Jewish people in Israel, Britain continued to expend considerable energy in preventing the entry of illegal Jewish immigrants. A Jewish Israeli working for CMJ has more recently put it thus: "The British didn't treat Jewish people especially badly at the end of the Mandate; they just began to treat them like the rest of the world does!"

The labour pains leading up to Israel's rebirth were severe and protracted, and it was not only the Jews who suffered. It was Jewish terrorists who massacred around 100 Arab villagers at Deir Yassin, just outside Jerusalem, as fighting escalated. Revenge was swift as 75 Jewish doctors and other medics were slaughtered in an attack on a convoy heading for the Hadassah Hospital.

The British Mandate formally ended on May 15 1948, the day after the declaration of the new state. Kelvin Crombie makes a strong case for the belief that Gallipoli (1915), seen at the time as a tragic waste of men with 8,000 Anzacs losing their lives, paved the way for the capture of Jerusalem and the eventual restoration of Israel. Had that battle been won, the war would likely have turned in another direction. Now a similar principle had been apparent during World War II. "As frightening as the prospect of a German-led invasion of Israel was, it was this period which provided tens of thousands of Jewish people with military training," Crombie writes. They reaped the benefits in subsequent wars of their own. After 1948, what had been known as the 'land between empires' was to become the land between the industrialised

West and the oil fields of Arabia; and "the land of conflict between those who adhere to the belief that Israel has been promised to the Jewish people and those who challenge this promise." As Crombie points out, it was "almost a forgotten land" until the Jews returned to live there.

Chapter 9

'Dragon' Attacks New-Born Nation!

The plain reason for the outbreak of the Arab-Israeli War was the fact that Arabs did not want a Jewish state in their neighbourhood. But its origins can be traced back some 4,000 years to the enmity between Isaac and Ishmael, both children of Abraham, the father of the Jewish race. Isaac was the 'son of promise' – that is, he was promised by God even though Abraham and his wife Sarah were well past the normal age of fertility – while Ishmael was born to Hagar, the couple's Egyptian servant, and was the result of manipulating the situation rather than believing the word of God. This explains, both on a physical and spiritual level, why the two are still bitter rivals. But it is not God's will – he longs for the reconciliation that can only be achieved through common recognition of the shed blood of Abraham's descendant, the Messiah, for our sins.

The 1948 war broke out on the very day Israel became a nation once again after nearly 2,000 years of dispersion. Jews had been returning to the Holy Land in droves since the 1880s, partly due to rising persecution in the countries of their adoption but also through encouragement by evangelical Christians and Jewish Zionists. The prophetic Scriptures spoke repeatedly of restoration to the land, and to the Lord, and many had been praying and working towards this end.

Britain had been given the awesome responsibility to fulfil its own promise by preparing a national homeland for the persecuted Jews. But as soon as it became clear that a

Jewish state was in the offing, Arab opposition mounted. Mobs rioted and Jews were mercilessly attacked, as is still happening today. It was no secret that Jerusalem's Mufti Haj Amin al-Husseini colluded with Hitler in plans to exterminate the Jews. Moreover, by World War II, Arab oil had also become an issue. Just as the German Fuehrer had no doubt taken courage from Neville Chamberlain's appeasement of Nazi ambitions, the Arabs will have been bolstered by their ability to get a major world power (Britain) to buckle under their pressure.

So, in flagrant defiance of a United Nations vote recognising the state of Israel (despite Britain's abstention), six Arab states immediately attacked the new-born nation – an action graphically portrayed in Revelation 12.4f which depicts a dragon (Satan) about to swoop on a new-born child, also fulfilled with Herod's killing of the innocents in a bid to murder the new King of Israel born in Bethlehem.

Correspondents had descended on the Holy Land in droves expecting to witness the birth and death of a state in rapid succession. Even such a military expert as Field Marshal Montgomery remarked at a press conference that "The Jews are done for!" From a natural military point of view, this view was of course quite understandable as little Israel was outnumbered by a ratio of 40:1 and most of her soldiers had been called from the fields, without armament matching that of their enemies.

Miraculously, however, Israel survived the onslaught and went on to rebuild the ancient ruins of a land that had been left desolate for millennia, though Jordan illegally annexed Judea, Samaria and Jerusalem's Old City. These, however, were re-captured in the Six-Day War of 1967, though they remain disputed territories (known as the West Bank) on the international political scene. It is important to note that Israel was not attacked because they were seen as occupying

'Palestinian land' or brutally treating 'Palestinians', for there were no such people. If anyone was known as Palestinian in the early life of modern Israel, it was the Jews who lived there. The motivation for attack was plainly – and still is – a denial of the Jewish state's right to exist.

As mentioned, the Holy Land was described by travellers as a "barren wasteland" in the late 19th century. But when Jews began resettling in numbers, Arabs from neighbouring countries effectively became economic migrants benefiting from jobs produced by expanding agricultural and other enterprises.

Politicians today keep talking of a 'two-state solution', but in reality this was achieved way back in 1922 when Churchill created Transjordan (now known as Jordan, east of the Jordan River) for the Arabs, in a bid to offset their vociferous opposition to British proposals for a new Israel. A further attempt to appease the Arabs was later made by offering territory west of the Jordan including Judea and Samaria, but this was rejected out of hand. So it was no solution then, and it is hard to understand how it can still be seen as the way to peace.

Political pawns in a Middle Eastern game of chess

So when did the Palestinian refugee crisis begin and what caused it? The problem was created by, and coincided with, the birth of modern Israel. But the popular understanding that the Jewish state sent them packing is a terrible distortion of the truth. The newly-reborn nation in fact urged its Arab residents to stay; the call for them to leave in haste came from the surrounding Arab countries in order to clear the way for a multi-pronged military attack designed to abort such nationhood and drive Israel into the sea. As a result, an estimated half-a-million Arabs fled in terror, with many subsequently housed in squalid refugee camps set up in

Jordan, Syria, Lebanon, Gaza and the West Bank, including East Jerusalem, where they continue to be used as political pawns in an ongoing propaganda campaign aimed at depicting the Jews as bullies.

British author Fred Wright reckons these refugees "must rate as some of the most unfortunate people in the modern world"[1] as, along with their descendants, the majority still live in temporary settlements. They are not, however, victims of Israel's hard-heartedness, but of the stubbornness and cunning of their fellow-Arab hosts, who could easily have absorbed them into their own communities, just as Israel has done for many of the 700,000 Jews[2] expelled at the same time from Arab countries. Jews of the dispersion who had made their home in North African and other Arab nations for centuries were thrown out (or persecuted) in response to the United Nations vote recognising Israel, but were quickly welcomed and absorbed by the fledgling state.

Meanwhile Jordan, Lebanon, Saudi Arabia, Egypt, Syria and Iraq refused to accommodate their Arab brethren, choosing rather to use them for a Middle Eastern 'game' of chess intended to checkmate Jewish aspirations, blaming Israel instead for a political mess that continues to this day. Put simply, the refugees are a creation of the Arab states surrounding Israel, yet much of the media would have you believe Israel was the culprit. But it is an upside-down world we live in today in which evil is called good, and good evil (see Isaiah 5.20). The absurdity of this phenomenon is highlighted by the fact that, as part of Britain's aid programme, an £18,000 a year stipend is paid (via the Palestinian Authority) to a couple of jailed Palestinians who stabbed a British woman and murdered her friend.[3]

So because the situation was not dealt with at the time, as Israel had done with her own refugees, the problem now involves some five million people, with the descendants of those first refugees also claiming a right of return to what they regard as their own land of 'Palestine'. Of course the unfortunate refugees had succumbed to the false hope of being able to return to a territory cleansed of Jews. But like so many previous attempts at Jewish annihilation, the planned genocide failed as a 'young David' overcame a 'Goliath' of six nations bent on their destruction, and would yet survive further wars against the odds. In fighting Israel over land promised to them by God, the result was inevitable. Speaking of Israel's restoration, the Lord declared through the prophet Amos: "I will plant Israel in their own land, never again to be uprooted..." (Amos 9.15).

But most Palestinians believe the lie that the land has been stolen from them, and a common perception is that the current wave of stabbings and shootings is borne of despair over general mistreatment and injustice. Whereas Hamas leader Ismail Haniyeh says this "cheapens the meaning of the struggle... What motivates the youths of the West Bank is the spirit of Jihad (Holy War)."[4] The real reason behind Palestinian terror, he says, is the 'liberation' of Jerusalem and replacing the State of Israel with 'Palestine'. In other words, a two-state solution is not seen as an option. They only want one state, and it is not Israel!

Readers may well wonder how Palestinians can get away with so much propaganda. But as *Israel Today* journalist Ryan Jones puts it, "many, if not most, Palestinians have no problem telling bald-faced lies in order to smear Israel and advance their own nationalist agenda. This is because Muslims are permitted to lie to 'infidels' in service to Islamic causes, a concept known as *taqiyya*."[5]

You decide who is telling the truth!

Armageddon – painting a picture of hope for the future

Before leaving the conflict surrounding the birth of modern Israel, I must share the amazing story of the colonel's wife who held the bullets for a machine-gun in a battle won without a shot fired.

Armageddon, biblical scene of the world's last great battle that will usher in the return of Jesus Christ, is no fictional location. It is a real place at Megiddo in northern Israel that has witnessed conflicts going back several millennia, but which has also inspired a series of priceless paintings. The works are the legacy of Lady Barbara Brassey, who died in her 99th year in 2010, and have been left in the custody of Wrexham-based TV and radio executive Gareth Littler.[6] Lady Brassey actually played a part in the little-remembered 1939 Battle of Armageddon (the Greek name for Megiddo, which overlooks the Plain of Jezreel) which, along with other battles already mentioned, also paved the way for the rebirth of Israel.

Yet if the Islamic jihadists who fled from the British forces at Megiddo had been successful, it could all have been so different. However, they have now re-emerged as perhaps the biggest threat, not only to Israel, but to world peace. For though Armageddon itself has since been quiet, wars and revolutions have broken out all over the Middle East, prompting fears of something much bigger and more brutal to come. Of great strategic importance, Megiddo guards a narrow pass on the ancient Egypt-Assyria trade route and is perhaps the most fought over place on earth. It was also where General Allenby's British Allied troops defeated the Turks in 1918 after taking Jerusalem without a shot fired.

But the paintings speak of hope, not war. The hands of the artist actually held the bullets with which to feed the machine gun aimed at the invading jihadists. Lady Brassey[7] was married to Col Campbell Westmoreland, who marched his battalion from Caesarea on the coast to face a hostile army at Megiddo. He lined his men up with their rifles and stationed his best 'Tommy' on the flat roof of a nearby building with a machine gun. Outnumbered and short of men, he asked his wife to feed the gun with the bullets. But miraculously, no shots were fired as, suddenly and inexplicably, the entire jihadist army turned and marched away. The war developed along different lines and in other theatres.

But, as Gareth Littler put it: "If that part of Palestine had fallen to a cohesive, organized jihadist army in 1939, no Jewish refugees could have passed through Haifa or Tel Aviv sea ports in the 1940s. The extraordinary battle helped pave the way for modern Israel. And in thanks to God for such a miracle, we have these marvellous paintings as a lasting legacy."

Barbara became a committed Christian in later life and the 'Armageddon Paintings' – depicting ten scenes from the Bible including Jesus' baptism, crucifixion, resurrection and return to earth at the end of the age – are seen as a prophetic sign that when Christ intervenes, peace is secured. Lady Brassey was a silver medal winner at the Royal Academy with works exhibited in London, Paris, America and South Africa, and this unique collection has been described as "priceless" by fine art valuer Peter Ashburner. The collection is expected to attract particular interest at a time when the sort of apocalypse envisaged by biblical prophets like Ezekiel and Daniel, and Jesus himself in the Book of Revelation, is becoming an ever-greater present reality.

Gareth says the message, both of the experience of Barbara at Armageddon that inspired the paintings and of the Scriptures themselves, is that it will not be Russia, as many Christians believe, that launches an all-out attack on Israel in the last days, but an alliance of Islamic jihadists. Muslim countries, he explains, have a history of recurring

Jihad (Holy War) in common – Islamic State arose 100 years after the massacre of millions of Armenians and others in a Turkish jihad. An apocalyptic scenario is rapidly developing before our eyes, but the solution lies with the Lord Jesus Christ, the prophet Isaiah's 'Prince of Peace', who will bring an end to warmongering as he turns swords into ploughshares and spears into pruning hooks (see Isaiah 2.4).

Gareth wonders, too, whether the 1939 battle could also be a prophetic picture of God intervening there again with massive power at the end of time, with victory again won without men firing a shot! Zechariah wrote: "A day of the Lord is coming when… I will gather all nations to Jerusalem to fight against it… Then the Lord will go out and fight against those nations..." (Zech 14.1-3).

"World leaders recognize a cataclysmic world war is now possible, but those who love God are reassured over Armageddon," says Gareth. "As things get worse, the world will struggle to find answers. But the good news of the Armageddon Paintings is that the Christian gospel holds the answer because Jesus rose from the dead and is coming back soon!"

Notes

[1] *Father, Forgive Us*, Fred Wright, Olive Press/Monarch Books pp 211/212.

[2] *Anzacs, Empires and Israel's Restoration*, Kelvin Crombie, Vocational Education and Training Publications.

[3] *Daily Mail* April 4 2016.

[4] *Israel Today*, March 2016.

[5] Ibid.

[6] Gareth Littler is a farmer, scientist and broadcaster who, as director of United Christian Broadcasters, spent 14 years building up the UCB television, radio and media company from humble beginnings.

[7] Her second marriage was to Lord Bernard Thomas Brassey, 2nd Baron of Apethorpe, Northamptonshire.

Chapter 10

Prayer that Won the War

Above all the preaching, plotting and political manoeuvring, there was surely no greater contribution to Israel's restoration than prayer. The saints of God had been praying for centuries towards this end, but there can have been few better examples of intercessory prayer that truly moved mountains than that of Welshman Rees Howells, founder of the Bible College of Wales. It has been said that World War II was won, not by our brave Spitfire pilots or the inspiring leadership of Churchill, but on the battlefield of prayer led by men like Howells who literally fought the enemy on their knees. It was in that vein that he and his students successfully steered us through the crisis of Dunkirk, when 335,000 British troops were trapped on the beaches as the Nazi war machine closed in on them.

In the years leading up to the war, their prayers began to be focused on national and international affairs as Howells came to see that Hitler was Satan's agent for preventing the gospel being preached to every creature. "The world became our parish and we were led to be responsible to intercede for countries and nations." His biographer Norman Grubb, in *Rees Howells – Intercessor*, writes: "From this time on, through all the years of the war, the whole college was in prayer every evening from 7pm to midnight, with only a brief interval for supper. They never missed a day. This was in addition to an hour's prayer meeting every morning, and very often at midday. There were many special periods when every day was given up wholly to prayer and fasting." Howells told his students: "Don't allow those young men at the Front to do more than you do here." Over the Dunkirk period, he spent four days alone with God "to battle through and, as others have testified, the crushing burden of those days broke his body. He literally laid down his life."

A year before the outbreak of war, Howells became burdened for Israel and the Jewish people, so much so that he stepped out in faith for a huge sum of money with which to purchase a large estate to house Jewish children who managed to escape Nazi-occupied Europe. Grubb writes that "it is remarkable now to see the fulfillment of the first stage of their prayer in the actual return of the Jews and the establishment of the State of Israel. How little there seemed any outward sign that this would come to pass, when the burden first came on his servant!" On September 7, 1938 he told his students: "I firmly believe the times of the Gentiles are drawing to a close, and the Jews must be back in their own land when the Master returns."

What Grubb refers to as "intense prayer" was also made over the November 1947 United Nations vote on whether to recognise Israel, during which they saw in faith "God's angels influencing those men in New York to work on behalf of God's people" and had full assurance of victory. When the vote was carried, the news was received with much rejoicing at the college as "one of the greatest days for the Holy Ghost in the history of these 2,000 years". But it is interesting (in the light of the growing reconciliation now being experienced between Jew and Arab) that Howells also received a burden for the Arabs, recognising that Abraham also loved Ishmael, and God had blessed him too.

Also making a significant contribution to Israel's restoration was Derek Prince, already mentioned as author of *Appointment in Jerusalem*, the dramatic story of his first wife Lydia. Born to British parents in India, Derek was educated in the classics at two of Britain's most prestigious institutions

– Eton College and Cambridge University. Serving with the British Army in World War II, he took a Bible with him to study 'as a work of philosophy'. But one night, alone in the barracks, he was confronted with the reality of Jesus Christ, and his life took a totally new direction. In time he became internationally recognised as one of the world's leading Bible expositors with a sharp prophetic insight into world events, especially as regards Israel, and while authoring dozens of books, his radio broadcasts reached much of the globe.

Following the death of Lydia, Derek married Ruth in 1978. An American, she had converted to Judaism when marrying her Jewish first husband in 1952, and discovered Jesus as her Messiah in 1970. She then emigrated to Jerusalem, where she met Derek and subsequently shared in his ongoing ministry of writing and intercession. CMJ's former USA director Dr Theresa Newell recalls the last time she saw Derek.

> It was at a service at Christ Church, Jerusalem, in August 1995. I was there to attend the International Conference of the Lausanne Consultation on Jewish Evangelism. The church was packed with visitors from around the world, as is often the case at CMJ's historic church in Jerusalem's Old City. Derek Prince and other Christ Church members led a powerful intercessory prayer group there during the 80s and 90s and he was a prolific writer on the topic of the power of prayer and fasting. On a recent trip to Israel, I walked with a friend who serves as a caretaker at the Christian cemetery in Jerusalem to see where Derek Prince is buried and to pay my respects. His books and teaching influenced an entire generation of believers and it is good that they are still available to readers today. His love for the Jewish people and his understanding of their place in God's plan of salvation ran deep in his life and were expressed wonderfully in all his books. And *Appointment*

in Jerusalem was a book which blessed me greatly as a new believer.

Another major influence on a Christian understanding of Israel was Lance Lambert, an anointed orator, Bible teacher and author as well as inspirational leader of intercessory prayer. He was particularly involved (along with Derek Prince) with *Christian Friends of Israel*. He, too, was known for his wisdom, wit and eloquence, which I experienced myself at a 1998 conference held in a Dorset cornfield. Of Jewish ancestry (his father and many members of his family died in the Holocaust), Lance grew up in Richmond, Surrey, and became a believer aged just twelve. He became an Israeli citizen in 1980 and died in Jerusalem in 2015, aged 84. Often referred to as 'a senior statesman of Israel', Lambert was a long-time friend of prominent Israeli leaders and an authority on the nation's Bible history. With a unique insight into the future, he shared a number of prophecies which are coming to pass in our day and, on the back cover of one of his books, *Battle for Israel* (Kingsway Publications), it is said of him that "never before has one man been allowed to enter into the confidence of Israelis to such an extent – Lambert, a Christian, welcomed and loved by Jews."

British preacher and author David Pawson has also contributed in no small way to a balanced biblical view of Middle Eastern affairs. He made a huge impact on me when addressing the subject of Israel at a 1980 convention of the Full Gospel Business Men's Fellowship International at Wembley in London. I was a relatively new Christian at the time with not much understanding of the situation. I can't remember the essence of what he said; I just know that it resonated powerfully within my heart, and when another speaker, Steve Lightle, implored his hearers to 'stand in the gap' for the Lord for the crucial times ahead, I stood up and somehow knew that it was a life-changing moment. I knew, for example, from thereon that the national newspaper for which I already had a vision must include fair in-depth coverage of the Middle East. Pawson was already pastor of a large Baptist church in Surrey and has since become world-renowned as an anointed speaker and author.

Another hugely influential figure is Richard Wurmbrand who, though not British, was a product of CMJ's mission to Jews, originally founded in England of course. Wurmbrand was a cause célèbre when I was 'growing up' as a Christian in the 1970s, with his book *Tortured for Christ* (Release International) inspiring a generation of believers. A Jewish atheist before turning to Christ, Wurmbrand spent 14 years in a Romanian prison, three of them in solitary confinement, while suffering brutal treatment at the hands of his Communist jailors. Though originally "a convinced atheist", he had no peace, and one day prayed for God to reveal himself to him, if indeed he did exist.

> During this time of inner turmoil, an old carpenter in a village high up in the mountains of Romania prayed like this: "My God, I have served you on earth and I wish to have my reward on earth as well as in heaven. And my reward should be that I should not die before I bring a Jew to Christ, because Jesus was from the Jewish people. But I am poor, old and sick. I cannot go around and seek a Jew. In my village there are none. Bring a Jew into my village and I will do my best to bring him to Christ." Something irresistible drew me to that village. I had no reason to go there. Romania has 12,000 villages, but I went to that one. Seeing I was a Jew, the carpenter courted me as never a beautiful girl had been courted. He saw in me the answer to his prayer and gave me a Bible to read.

It wasn't just words, however, that won Richard's heart, but "flames of love fired by the man's prayers". Wurmbrand became a notable evangelist, but paid dearly for the privilege of preaching Christ in the Communist world.

A man who greatly influenced me as a result of a lengthy interview I had with him in 2009, when he was CMJ's UK chief, was Robin Aldridge, a former primary school headteacher. Sharing his journey to faith, he said he kept being invited to a Baptist church by a member of staff. He and his wife Sue eventually ran out of excuses and visited the church where he recalls an "uncanny feeling that the pastor knew everything about me and was preaching to me personally. That set us off on a journey in which I personally tried to think my way through to God. But then, during a weekend event at a Bible College in England's Peak District, I had an overwhelming experience of Jesus and it completely broke me."

Sue came to her own decision for Christ and they got baptized together in 1982. Then, during the 1991 Gulf War, Sue was very worried about the conflict between Iraq and Kuwait and asked the pastor if they could host a prayer meeting for the purpose. Many came, and when they heard on the 9 p.m. news that Iraq had fired scud missiles into Israel, Robin and Sue had a revelation. "At that moment the scales fell off from our eyes," Robin recalled – "that what that war was all about was Israel and the Jewish people – and God gave us a burden for Israel."

Chapter 11

Light in the Darkness

Thank goodness for the world statesmen (and women) we have produced over the years. Unfortunately, their wise counsel was not always sought. In the case of Churchill, his repeated warnings to Parliament of the dangers of German re-armament and the rise of Nazism during the 1930s went largely unheeded until it was too late. He was then invited to help sort out the mess created by his appeasing colleagues by stepping in as wartime Prime Minister, and what a terrific job he did! However, there is no doubt that Britain could, and should, have acted sooner – especially with regard to saving Jewish lives in Nazi-occupied Europe. We betrayed God's chosen people, and have their blood on our hands as a result. Even after the sickening reality of the Holocaust was revealed to a world shuddering in shock, we did little to help survivors start afresh in their ancient homeland. But there were flickers of light in the darkness, one of which involved a future Prime Minister and world leader, Margaret Thatcher.

Mrs Thatcher was both revered and reviled for her forthright leadership of Britain from 1979-1990. Whatever you think of her, she was undoubtedly a woman who commanded great respect among world leaders. I have no doubt that the success of her career was in no small measure due to the fact that she blessed the seed of Abraham. Her proudest moment, she had said, was in saving a Jewish teenager from the Holocaust. In 1938 Edith Muhlbauer, a 17-year-old Austrian, sent a letter to Muriel Roberts, her pen pal and Margaret's older sister, asking if the Roberts family could help her escape. The Nazis had started rounding up Jews from Vienna and Edith knew it was just a matter of time before she would be among them.

Grantham grocer Alfred Roberts had neither the time nor money to bring Edith to their home. So Muriel, 17, and Margaret, then only 12, decided to try raising money themselves and asking the local Rotary Club to help. They duly succeeded in bringing Edith to England where she stayed for the next two years before joining relatives in South America. Edith apparently slept in Margaret's room and Mrs Thatcher later wrote in her memoirs: "She was tall, beautiful, and evidently from a well-to-do family. But most important, she told us what it was like to live as a Jew under an anti-Semitic regime. One thing Edith reported particularly stuck in my mind. The Jews, she said, were being made to scrub the streets."

In 1995, after Edith had been located in Brazil, she told audiences: "Never hesitate to do whatever you can, for you may save a life." At the time of writing, she was a grandmother in Sao Paulo who said she owed her life and that of her children and grandchildren to Margaret Thatcher's family. Mrs Thatcher, meanwhile, went on to represent the North London parliamentary constituency of Finchley which included some very Jewish areas such as Golders Green, and she worked tirelessly on their behalf throughout her career.

When she visited Yad Vashem (the Holocaust Museum in Jerusalem) during a historic first visit to Israel by a British Prime Minister in 1986, she was visibly shaken as she stood in front of a photo of a German soldier shooting a Jewish mother and child. "It is so terrible," she said. "Everyone should come and see it so that they never forget. I am not quite sure whether the new generation really knows what we are fighting against."

On Israel's security, she said: "Israel must never be expected to jeopardise her security; if she was ever foolish enough to do so and then suffered for it, the backlash against both honest brokers and Palestinians would be immense – 'land for peace' must also bring peace."

Following her death, Israeli Prime Minister Netanyahu said: "She was truly a great leader, a woman of principle, of determination, of conviction, of strength; a woman of greatness. She was a staunch friend of Israel and the Jewish people. She inspired a generation of political leaders."

Jewish debt to British Christians

Another great unsung hero of the hour was Sir Nicholas Winton, who was knighted for his extraordinary efforts only towards the end of his long life – he died at 106. Winton, a lawyer, heard about the *Kindertransport* project to rescue children from Nazi-occupied Czechoslovakia in 1938, and became personally responsible for rescuing 669 of them, forging passports and even bribing Nazi officials to get the youngsters to safety – and many of those who took them in were Christians. As a result, generations of people – almost 7,000 of some of the world's greatest doctors, lawyers, teachers and inventors – owe their lives to the act of one man's efforts to help Jewish children escape the Nazis.

Among those who benefited from this scheme, and who was profoundly grateful to Christians for their help, was Lord Weidenfeld, who also died recently at the advanced age of 96. He became a prominent British Jew and took the opportunity of the Syrian refugee crisis to repay Christians for the way they have helped his people. Believing Islamic State to be more evil than the Nazis, the publishing magnate set up a fund to help rescue Christian families caught up in the conflict.

After escaping from Vienna as Hitler drove his family

from Austria in 1938, he found himself in London surviving on handouts. In due time he founded the publishing house Weidenfeld & Nicolson, was made a peer of the realm, became a counsellor to heads of state and even counted himself a friend of the Pope (John Paul II). "And I owe all this to one act of Christian charity," he wrote in a major article for *The Mail on Sunday*.[1] "In my time of greatest need, a family of evangelical Christians, Plymouth Brethren, took me in."

It was a debt he believed he could never repay, but the time had now come to try. With Christmas (it was December) being a season of "goodwill to all men", there was no better moment to speak out about the fund he had established "which unites the power of the Christian Church and Jewry to rescue Christians from Syria". Relying on Christian charity *Barnabas Fund* to deal with the logistics, his Jewish network committed to raise money to help pay the bills. Quoting Pope John Paul II, who used to say that "the Jew is the elder brother of the Church," he concluded by saying: "This Christmas it is time for us to look after our younger siblings."

UK Christians rally behind Israel

Few could have imagined that anti-Semitism would still be a major problem 70 years after the liberation of Auschwitz. But the year in question witnessed two shocking terrorist attacks on Paris, with Jews specifically targeted on both occasions, along with a wave of stabbings and shootings in Israel itself. One incident occurred on Christmas Eve at Jaffa Gate, Jerusalem, just yards from Christ Church, where they were celebrating the birth of the Messiah who came to bring peace to a troubled world and where, ironically, they steadfastly work towards reconciling Arab and Jew through the atoning sacrifice of Jesus.

But even as the UK marks Holocaust Memorial Day in January each year, we too are witnessing an ongoing rise in anti-Semitic incidents necessitating armed guards having to be deployed to schools in London's Jewish community. But is the Church as a whole rallying to the support of those who are once more threatened with genocide, as they were under the Nazis? Do they even care?

Here is the stark reality of what is facing the Jewish people today: Iran is fast developing nuclear weapons with which to "wipe out" Israel (in the words of the Ayatollahs and Iranian presidents) and, ominously in the eyes of many, the Russian Bear has now established a foothold in the region. The current spat between Shiite Iran and Sunni Saudi Arabia further adds to the tension, and Gaza-based Hamas is repeatedly firing rockets into the Jewish state while Lebanon-based Hezbollah continues to pose a serious threat on its northern border. Brutal Islamic State are also stalking the area while the Palestinian Authority incites its people to murder and mayhem, and some Westerners are engaged in a boycott of Israeli goods on the pretext that they are oppressive occupiers of land not their own. But the truth is that, in most cases, Jews are being attacked simply because they are Jews, not for political or economic reasons. With all this in mind, UK Christians who can see what is happening are trying to draw the attention of a generally uncaring public to the plight of Jews everywhere.

One of them, John Fieldsend, whose parents perished at Auschwitz, was also taken in by a kind Christian couple after being rescued by Nicholas Winton. He became a follower of Jesus and a full-time preacher, but it could all have been so different. On a visit to the Children's Memorial at Yad Vashem, he recalls: "As we listened to the names of the children being read out on an endlessly looping tape – which took several days to go round – I realized that had my journey from Czechoslovakia been delayed by only about five weeks, my name would have been on that tape! It was a very dramatic experience..."

Israeli Prime Minister Netanyahu's account of his own family history, shared in a United Nations speech, perfectly illustrates the necessity for such memorial days. After being beaten senseless by a group of anti-Semitic hoodlums at a railway station in the heart of Europe, his grandfather Nathan promised himself that, if he lived, he would take his family to the Jewish homeland and help build a future for the Jewish people.

Six million Jews perished in the gas chambers, but the nightmares of the survivors live on while new generations face fresh threats. When will it stop? We have so much for which to thank them – they gave us the Bible, on the foundations of which we have built a great civilization. And they gave us Jesus, Saviour of both Jews and Gentiles who put their trust in Him, who said: "Whatever you did for one of the least of these brothers of mine, you did for me." (Matthew 25.40)

'Atheists at the heart of the problem'

As British Christians remembered the Holocaust on January 27, 2016 – marking the day in 1945 when Auschwitz was liberated – they were reminded that it was spawned by godlessness and the rejection of faith. Steven Jaffe, a member of the UK's Jewish Board of Deputies, was addressing a largely Christian audience at a church in Sheffield, Yorkshire.

He said the exodus from Egypt was immediately followed by the battle with Amalek, who had no reason to attack Israel. There was no territorial dispute or history of conflict, for example. And they attacked the sick and the elderly – those who were most vulnerable. (See Deuteronomy 25.17-18.) "The conflict with Amalek is not over," he said. Amalek denied God and his power in the same way the Nazis did, and the latter mirrored their lack of mercy. Jaffe recalled that

Britain's former Chief Rabbi, Lord Sachs, was once asked where God was during the Holocaust, to which he is said to have replied: "Where was man?"

My worry is that the growing influence of rank atheism in Britain and Europe will have a bearing on the future of anti-Semitism. The poisonous view that God does not exist naturally leads to godless behaviour and thought, even among those previously tutored in godly ways. The result is that even some who claim to have faith, and who perhaps stand in pulpits, start believing the lie that is proclaimed so often through almost every strand of media. It is indeed frustrating that, as fast as we spread word about the horrors of the Holocaust, vowing that it should never be repeated, the vile infestation of anti-Semitism creeps into every crack and crevice of a broken society as the walls of a Judeo-Christian civilization come crashing down around us.

Among the organisers of the Sheffield event was Ginnie White, whose mother Stella was roughed up by Oswald Mosley's fascists as a child growing up in London's East End where she was also once jeered at as a "dirty Jew". In today's Britain, hatred of Jews is generally not expressed openly, but often takes the form of a loathing of Israel, so that the very mention of the Jewish state is enough to raise the hackles not only of the politically-aware man in the street, but of the semi-biblically aware man in the pew.

As Steven told the Sheffield church, such loathing cannot be explained in rational terms. But he was spot on target, I believe, in linking the phenomenon with a society that has thrown God out of the window. Pledges of never letting it happen again are not enough, in my opinion; without a recovery of faith in the God of Israel, there can be no guarantee that another holocaust won't take place.

Even as I write, Iran is boasting of a nuclear deal that "has provided an historic opportunity to... face threats posed by the Zionist entity".[2] As we have discussed, the former Grand Mufti of Jerusalem, Haj Amin al-Husseini, collaborated with Hitler, thus setting the stage for today's Jihad against Israel.[3] Yet, bizarrely, former Iranian president Mahmoud Ahmadinejad and current Palestinian leader Mahmoud Abbas have both publicly denied that the Holocaust ever took place.[4]

Steven Jaffe himself, through the launch in 2015 in the neighbouring city of Leeds of the *Shalom Declaration*, committing to pray for the peace of Jerusalem and fight against anti-Semitism, is sending out a clear message of Christian support for Britain's Jewish community. "There isn't a corner of the British Isles that the *Shalom Declaration* has not been signed," he said.

Making nonsense of campaigns to boycott Israel, he pointed out that one in six of the drugs and medicine dispensed through Britain's famous health service have either been manufactured or developed in Israel. On the faith front, we were told that "there are more Jews learning the Torah today in Israel than at any time in our history". All of which is preparing them well for the great event we are perhaps soon to witness, when Jesus reveals himself on a grand scale to his brothers in the flesh. Though many Jews quite understandably have a problem with this, especially with the Holocaust in mind, the key is forgiveness.

British television viewers were treated to a remarkable Channel 4 documentary, *The girl who forgave the Nazis*, recounting the story of how Hungarian Jew Eva Kor, a former inmate of Auschwitz, has publicly forgiven Oskar Groenig, the death camp's former accountant, who was recently sentenced to four years in jail for his part in the Nazis' evil scheme. Eva and her twin sister Miriam were experimented on by the infamous Dr Josef Mengele, but survived the camp, though Miriam died in 1993, possibly through the effects of the experiments. Eva said: "It's time to forgive, but not forget… I believe that forgiveness is such a powerful thing... and I want everybody to help me sow these seeds of peace throughout the world."

This takes amazing courage. But it is worth remembering that Jesus, our Messiah, made the first move when he prayed, as he died in agony on a cross in Jerusalem: "Father, forgive them, for they do not know what they are doing" (Luke 23.34). When the Jewish patriarch Joseph revealed himself to his brothers, he had already long since forgiven them for acting treacherously against him.

I conclude this chapter with the testimony of Israeli General Yossi Peled, who was also spared from the Holocaust by a courageous Christian family who took him in and raised him as their own until his mother returned from the death camps to claim him. He is now the Israeli chairman of Jerusalem's Friends of Zion Museum, the brainchild of American Messianic Jew Mike Evans, built to honour brave Christians who have risked all for God's chosen people over the years. Mike quotes Gen Peled as saying:

> Facing the man-made horrors, the acts of madness and terror of the Holocaust, there were also people who stood up to all of that, like points of light in the midst of all that darkness. The Friends of Zion Museum…conveys this precise message of hope and the ability to act against evil even in times of extreme difficulties…and is a dream come true for those who wanted to cherish the Righteous Among the Nations (Gentiles specially honoured by Jews for coming to their aid). In the past year, millions around the world have been introduced to the museum... and it is an honour to commemorate those who risked their lives in order to save the lives of others.

Notes

[1] Christians saved me from the Nazis…now I must save them from an even greater evil – *The Mail on Sunday*, December 20, 2015.
[2] Iranian Foreign Minister Mohammad Javad Zarif speaking in Beirut, August 12 2015.
[3] David Soakell, Christian Friends of Israel's Watching Over Zion newsletter, January 21 2016.
[4] Ibid.

Chapter 12

A Suitcase Tells Ten Thousand Stories

A pile of battered old suitcases act as props to a memorial of a very harrowing time for thousands of Jewish children at the outbreak of World War II. After being snatched from the jaws of almost certain death in the extermination camps of Nazi Germany, they will undoubtedly have been left extremely traumatised by the parting from their parents. Few of those innocent victims could have sensed that it was to be more than a temporary break. There is a note attached to one of the cases – a particularly large trunk – explaining why its owner had been reluctant to part with it.

In donating it to the Holocaust Centre and Museum at Laxton, near Newark in Nottinghamshire, England, she recalled how lovingly her mother had packed it, and how it became her most treasured possession because she never saw her again. It left me in tears as I contemplated the pain of that young child, and so many others like her, who had been torn from their mums and dads in a desperate bid to save them.

The cases were at the end of *The Journey*, a hugely impressive exhibition vividly recounting what it must have been like for children caught up in the *Kindertransport* operation which brought some ten thousand youngsters from German-occupied Europe to be placed with British families, and in which Sir Nicholas Winton played such a significant role. But before the journey to England, conducted in a very realistic train carriage with the passing scenery whizzing by, you are led through a typical Jewish boy's experience of what it must have been like living in Germany in the late 1930s. The sights and sounds of a typical street, complete with clanking trams, are seen through the window of his parents' apartment and you are taken into a schoolroom where he explains via a video screen how he felt when his best friend no longer wished to associate with him because he was Jewish. It is heart-rending stuff, especially when he learns that he is to be taken to England, away from his parents and everything he had known. There was even a special place to hide in the shop owned by his father, a tailor, and the exhibition was really brought home to me a short while later when I watched *The Book Thief*, a powerful movie focused on a German family who kept a Jewish man hidden for much of the war.

Yvonne Franklin, one of many Holocaust survivors who give regular talks at the centre, recalled her profound shock over the denial of Nazi horrors when she took her sons to the place in the south of France where she and her family had been holed up during the war, protected by the Resistance fighters. When she expressed her surprise that there was no evidence of that dreadful time, or of the brave efforts of those who risked their lives to shield them from the Gestapo – perhaps in the form of some memorial or plaque – the explanation given was that the events were merely legend!

That is why memorials are so important, because people soon forget, or would rather not remember, and history then repeats itself, which unfortunately is already happening in the Ukraine and elsewhere where, once more, Jews get the blame when things start going wrong in society. Thankfully, they do now have a homeland of their own, which was not the case in the thirties, but even in Israel they are not safe because terrorists and their sponsors constantly threaten their very existence.

As the credits rolled at the end of *The Book Thief*, with my wife and I both dabbing our tear-filled eyes with tissues, I caught sight of a decidedly unmoved moviegoer – slouching in his chair, surrounded by popcorn liberally strewn all over the floor, while he messed about with his mobile. It was the perfect picture of the heartless, ruthless, uncaring world we see all around us that would let it all happen again – if it was up to them!

German sisters pray as persecution continues

Nearly 80 years after *kristallnacht* – the night of officially sanctioned vandalism of Jewish businesses in Germany – the unprovoked persecution of God's ancient people continues. Anti-Semitic attacks are occurring all over Europe, but even in Israel, the supposed safe haven which rose from the ashes of the Holocaust that followed November 9, 1938 (also known as *Reichsprogromnacht*), individual Jews and their families innocently going about their daily lives are being mercilessly stabbed and shot at close range by terrorists justifying their cruelty on the basis of fighting a 'holy war'.

Having repeatedly threatened to wipe Israel off the map, a nuclear-armed Iran would pose an obvious danger not only to Israel but to Western civilisation itself, yet few asked why an American President presided over a deal seen only as putting off the evil day. Fortunately, Israel's Prime Minister Binyamin Netanyahu made it his business to point this out, but the rest of the world seems to think it has nothing to do with them. Now Britain is in danger of repeating history with the strong message of support Parliament sent to the Palestinian Authority over its quest for state recognition.

I was recently reminded of historic events in Europe as I shared time in prayer and conversation with a lovely British-based German lady, Sister Thekla, who has previously spoken of her shame at the suffering caused by her nation through the Holocaust and warns that today's church is in danger of repeating history. "In the not-too-distant future we Christians will all be challenged about our relationship to Israel," she told a conference in 2014. "Will we once more be silenced? Israel is once again hated by the nations, which is a picture of our Lord Jesus, who was despised and rejected of men. We are called to pray for Israel. They need love, borne out of repentance, the only kind that will open their hearts. We have often not presented the true image of Jesus to them.

"It grieves me what my nation has done, especially to the Jewish people. We had touched the apple of God's eye and saw God's judgment poured out on our nation as a result," she said, referring to the repeated bombing of Darmstadt which prompted Basilea Schlink, a local resident, to found the *Evangelical Sisterhood of Mary*, dedicated to reconciliation with the Jewish people.

One 1944 attack on Darmstadt killed 10 per cent of its inhabitants and made 60 per cent of its population homeless. Mother Schlink and a group of fellow Christians wept as they came under deep conviction of the terrible sin committed by Germany, and subsequently went to Israel to volunteer their services as nurses while seeking forgiveness for the persecution of their people dating back to the time of the Crusades.

"It is a painful memory, but I confess these crimes," Sister Thekla told the York conference. "If the German community had stood up as one man, the Nazis would not have been at such liberty to pursue their schemes. Where was the Christian church?"

I also renewed acquaintance with Sister Glory, a British member of the order with a Methodist background, who has said that Britain had blood on their hands concerning Israel. A massacre of Jews took place in York in 1190 and Jews were expelled from Britain a century later before being welcomed back at the time of Oliver Cromwell through the influence of the *Pilgrim Fathers*, a radical Christian group who were themselves hounded out of the country before emerging as the founding fathers of the United States.

Indeed, Bible-believing Christians like the *Pilgrim Fathers* and their spiritual successors have been consistent friends of Israel, playing a pivotal role in the return of God's chosen people to the Holy Land. But, as we have seen, Britain reneged on its pledge of support for a Jewish national home by dividing the land and acting treacherously to appease the Arabs while forcing the Jews to disarm. Many trying to escape the Holocaust were turned back. "We betrayed the greatest trust ever given to a nation," Sister Glory said.

In experiencing the fulfilment of Genesis 12.3 (that those who bless the seed of Abraham will themselves be blessed, while those who curse her will come under judgment), Britain has suffered the loss of her empire along with increasing decadence within the nation itself. As former British Prime Minister Benjamin Disraeli said: "The Lord deals with the nations as the nations deal with the Jews."

In an address on this subject given in Berlin in 2006, the order's Sister Joela said that, from his birth to his death, Jesus was inseparably linked with his people, the Jews. "We have been happy to take his mercies and blessings for ourselves, and have left the judgments and curses for his people," she said. The New Covenant in Jesus' blood was originally made with Jews, not with Gentiles (Jeremiah 31.31), she pointed out, adding that many had been blinded to important issues by selective interpretation of the Bible. There was little acknowledgement or recognition, for example, of chapters 9 to 11 of Paul's letter to the Romans, which deals with God's wonderful long-term plan for the Jewish people. Now, not just one nation, but a number of Israel's neighbours, have unequivocally declared their intent to pursue a 'final solution'. "And this time no-one can claim not to have known anything about it."

Sister Joela is convinced that, even after all these years, God is still waiting for the repentance of many Christians in Germany. In a speech to the German parliament on January 27, 2006, holocaust survivor Professor Ernst Cramer summed up the horrors he witnessed with the statement: "The thing that shocked me most at the time was the almost total silence of the Christian churches."

Various initiatives have in recent years uncovered further details concerning the active involvement of many sections of the established Protestant Church in Germany (Landeskirche) with a 'De-Judaization Institute' in Eisenach. They published a People's New Testament, hymn book and catechism from which every trace of the Jewish roots of Christianity had been eliminated.

Echoing the question of the Wise Men following the star to Bethlehem, Sister Joela asked: "Where is the King of the Jews?" Very prophetically in light of current events, she answered: "With his people! With his people in the thick of war, terrorism and disaster; in the midst of sin and injustice; at the focal point of world interest; at the centre of the hatred; in the midst of slander and contempt – that is where we will find him. The worldwide hatred towards God will be increasingly vented on those who have a living relationship with the God of the Bible and want to remain faithful to him. Therefore, in the final stages of world history, Jews and Christians will come under fire together. So let us give Jesus, our Lord and King, the answer borne of our love for him, and join together in making the commitment: 'Your people will be my people' (Ruth 1:16)."

The quotes from Sister Joela have been taken from the booklet *Where is the King of the Jews?* published in Darmstadt, Germany, by the Evangelical Sisterhood of Mary. See www.kanaan.org

Chapter 13

More Heroes of the Holocaust

Britain and other nations still mark Holocaust Memorial Day each year on January 27, the date in 1945 when the notorious death camp at Auschwitz was liberated by the Red Army.

Israel itself has since risen from the ashes of that dreadful scourge that wiped out six million European Jews but, as we have seen, they are still under dire threat from enemies on all sides while attacks on synagogues and other Jewish centres are still being carried out in the 'civilised' West.

The fragile borders to which the United Nations expect Israel to agree (just nine miles wide in places) have for good reason been described by politicians as 'Auschwitz lines' because they leave the Jewish state highly vulnerable to attack from neighbouring states who have repeatedly threatened to drive them into the sea.

It was also in January 1945 that one of the most heroic accounts of the war took place. But the incredible story has only recently surfaced because the hero concerned never spoke about it.

The truth was finally unearthed by his granddaughter when asked to focus on a family member as part of a college assignment. Her widowed grandmother gave her the diary kept by her husband during his time in a prisoner-of-war camp which revealed the astonishing fact that, by standing up to the German commandant, Master Sgt Roddie Edmonds, of Knoxville, Tennessee, had saved the lives of 200 American Jews.

As the highest-ranking officer there, Edmonds was made

responsible for the camp's 1,292 American GIs, 200 of whom were Jewish. Then one day the Germans ordered all Jewish POWs to report outside their barracks the following morning. Knowing what awaited them – being moved to a slave labour camp at the very least – he decided to resist the directive, ordering all his men to fall out the following morning.

The commandant, Major Siegmann, duly ordered Edmonds to identify the Jewish soldiers, to which the sergeant responded: "We are all Jews here."

Holding his pistol to Edmonds' head, the commandant repeated the order. But the sergeant – a devout Christian – refused.

"According to the Geneva Convention, we only have to give our name, rank and serial number. If you shoot me, you will have to shoot all of us, and after the war you will be tried for war crimes," Edmonds had said, according to one of the men saved that day.

Edmonds' pastor son Chris regards all of them as heroes as they could easily have identified the Jews among them to save their skin. But they all stood together.

It was some 70 years later that Roddie Edmonds was posthumously awarded the *Yehi Or* (Let there be light) Award by the Jewish Foundation for the Righteous. He has also been honoured by Jerusalem's Yad Vashem Holocaust Museum as 'righteous among the nations'.[1]

But as Jews were herded into cattle trucks for transporting to death camps, there weren't many Roddies about who dared to speak up and stand up on their behalf. These days, where controversial issues are concerned, leaders still prefer to keep their heads below the proverbial parapet while remaining 'impartial'. But there is a time when we must take sides. We must choose between life and death, between God and evil. If we claim to be Christian, we have no option.

"Neutrality is only an illusion," writes Robert Stearns. "Those who are not for God are against Him. (See Matthew 12.30a.) The German public's unfortunate legacy during World War II lies not in what they did in response to their despotic leader and his horrendous practices, but in what they did not do."[2]

This did not apply, however, to Hans Scholl and his sister Sophie, young Christians who led the White Rose leaflet campaign of resistance, for which they paid with their lives. Prophetically, they asked the question: "Who among us has any conception of the dimensions of shame that will befall us and our children when one day the veil has fallen from our eyes and the most horrible of crimes... reach the light of day?"[3]

Stearns also points out that, when the Nazis invaded European nations, many monarchs vacated their thrones and fled. But King Christian X stayed in Denmark as he defied the bullies. Thanks to his example, most Danish Jews survived the war.[4]

Princess Alice, the Queen's mother-in-law, has also been recognized by Jerusalem's Yad Vashem Holocaust Museum as 'righteous among the nations' for saving a Jewish family during the war, and is buried on the Mount of Olives.

As Princess of Greece, she hid Jewish widow Rachel Cohen and two of her five children in her home. Rachel's husband had in 1913 helped King George I of Greece, in return for which the king offered him any service he could perform, should he ever need it. When the Nazi threat emerged, his son recalled this promise and appealed to the Princess, who duly honoured her father's pledge. Prince Charles finally fulfilled a long-standing wish to visit his grandmother's grave.[5]

It is interesting in this respect that Prince Charles has compared the dangers facing minority faith groups across the world today with the "dark days of the 1930s".[6]

The Queen herself is a wonderful example of someone who is prepared to make an uncompromising stand for faith and truth, declaring in her Christmas message to the nation: "Jesus Christ lived in obscurity for much of his life and was maligned and rejected by many, though he had done no wrong. Millions now follow his teaching and find in him the guiding light of their lives. I am one of them..."

Are we, like the Queen, courageous enough to tell the entire world that we are followers of Jesus and, as such, will do all we can to stand up to the evil that lurks in every dark corner of our land?

Roddie Edmonds was prepared to die for 200 Jewish men. Abraham was prepared to sacrifice his son Isaac. But the greatest sacrifice of all was when Yeshua (Hebrew for *Jesus*), "though he had done no wrong", laid down his life for both Jews and Gentiles on a stake outside the walls of Jerusalem's Old City after being "led like a lamb to the slaughter" during the Passover feast (Isaiah 53.7). He bought our pardon; he paid the price.

Notes

[1] *Gateway News* (South Africa), December 1, 2016, originally published by *The Times of Israel*.

[2] *The Cry of Mordecai* by Robert Stearns (Destiny Image).

[3] Ibid.

[4] Ibid.

[5] *Torch magazine, Christians United for Israel – UK,* Dec 2016-Feb 2017.

[6] *Saltshakers* December 24, 2016, quoting *Premier Online*.

TESTIMONIES

Chapter 14

Jewish Pop Star Finds Joy in Jesus

Just as the 'swinging sixties' started to gain momentum, a Jewish teenager from the East End of London took the pop world by storm with a string of hits. Her first – *Don't Treat Me Like a Child* – was appropriate enough as Helen Shapiro was only 14 at the time (1961) and it reached No 3 in the charts. By early 1963 she was bigger than *The Beatles* – for a time. They actually accompanied her on a tour of the UK as her support act; she was the main attraction.

She recalls with affectionate nostalgia the banter she shared on the bus with John, Paul, George and Ringo, and it was during this tour, in February 1963, that *Please, Please Me* became the Fab Four's first No 1. Helen also made No 1 around this time with her classic upbeat number *Walking Back to Happiness*,[1] but says the lyrics of the song were not fulfilled until August 26, 1987 – over twenty years later – when she found Jesus, as she told a Yorkshire audience in 2015. For someone who associated Christians with persecutors of her people, it was quite an amazing turnaround. She had been confused and upset when, as a child in the school playground, someone yelled at her: "You killed Jesus Christ!" (This is of course a common misconception about Jews, especially among those untutored in the Scriptures, which make it clear that Christ *had* to die as the spotless Lamb of God paying for the sins of the world. He had offered himself of his own accord to be nailed to a cross.)

Helen duly developed her own system of beliefs after turning to mediums and spiritists, believing that God was involved in all those things. But then, soon after her 40th birthday, she no longer believed it and began questioning the very existence of God. She was in the midst of this crisis when her musical director (who was unaware of it) gave her a book to read, *Betrayed* by Stan Telchin. It was about a respectable member of a Jewish community who was suddenly faced with a daughter announcing that she believed Jesus was the Messiah of Israel. He duly set out to prove her wrong and ended up becoming a believer himself!

Helen began studying the many prophecies of the promised Messiah in the Jewish Bible (what Christians refer to as the Old Testament) and was astonished at how accurately they seemed to be fulfilled in Jesus (*Yeshua* in Hebrew). These included references to a virgin birth in Bethlehem while the description of the suffering servant in Isaiah 53 was surely a picture of the crucifixion, despite having been written some 600 years earlier. "Isaiah 53 was about how He took our sins… I was gobsmacked. And Daniel prophesied that the Messiah had to die before the temple was destroyed. It all seemed to point to Jesus."

So now she ventured to read "the chunk on the end I'm not supposed to read. And taking my courage in both hands, I opened the New Testament." She wondered if she would discover "anti-Jewish poison" in view of the track record of the professing church, which had committed unspeakable crimes against her people. "No wonder we don't come running towards this Jesus."

She started at the beginning – Matthew's gospel – and was surprised to find "the most Jewish thing outside the Old Testament" – the genealogy of Jesus which included a list of all the names from which Messiah must come. "Did you know the New Testament is Jewish?" she asked the audience. "It was written by Jewish men about the most famous Jew of all, and they were living in the land of Israel according to the Law of Moses. Jesus rose up out of the pages to me and I fell in love with him. I was so taken with him. He looked at people's hearts and saw all the rubbish and yet still loved them. Even in his agony he came out with gracious, comforting words. I saw that he was fulfilling one Messianic prophecy after another."

Just to make sure the English translators had not twisted anything to suit their purposes, she got hold of a Bible (the *Tenach*, or Old Testament to Christians) from a Jewish shop to check that it included the same Messianic prophecies. "Blow me: there they were in all their glory. I was so relieved." Back to the New Testament, she read through the four Gospels. "By the end of John I knew without a shadow of doubt that Jesus was the fulfilment of every Messianic prophecy; that he was the Jewish Messiah."

She contacted her musical director and his wife, bombarded them with questions, realised that she had been deceived by her dabbling with the occult and, at 10.30pm on August 26 1987, gave her life to Jesus. "There were no lightning flashes, but somewhere inside I knew that I knew, and that there was no turning back. The Creator and sustainer of the universe came to live in my life. I didn't get religion. I got Jesus, and I love him."

She had one further question and wrote to Stan Telchin, the author of the book that had started things off for her, asking: "Will I stop being Jewish by following Jesus?"

"Of course not," he replied. "You will be fulfilling your Jewishness. He's coming back as the Lion of the Tribe of Judah."

Acknowledging that God still has a plan for the nation of Israel, Helen emphasised that both Jew and Gentile find salvation only through the blood of Jesus. Though we are born physically, our spirits are dead because of man's sin and rebellion against God. That is why we need to be born again. God established the system of animal sacrifices to demonstrate that only through the shedding of the blood of an innocent substitute can a sinner be saved.

They were pointers to the once-for-all sacrifice that Jesus became that day on the cross in Jerusalem when he shed his blood for the sins of the world. That is why he came.[2]

Notes

[1] *Walking back to happiness* is also the title of Helen Shapiro's autobiography, published by Harper Collins.

[2] Personally, I owe an enormous debt to another Helen, also Jewish, who was effectively my spiritual mother in my early days as a Christian in the 1970s. Helen McIntosh, who always referred to herself as a 'completed Jew' rather than a Christian, gave her life to Jesus at a Billy Graham crusade in London in 1954. When I found the Lord in 1972, she was leading a 'nursery class' for new believers and those seeking answers under the direction of the the Rev John Stott, a legendary evangelical pastor, evangelist and Bible expositor who was Rector of All Souls, Langham Place, in central London. Helen taught me with great insight and depth which provided a solid foundation for my life of faith, complemented of course by the anointed preaching of John Stott himself and my own Bible study. Appropriately I suppose, in view or her eternal spiritual influence, I also insured my life with Helen, who was a sales representative for *Sun Life of Canada*!

Chapter 15

Pentecost Power for Service

A Jewish follower of Jesus was having second thoughts about being ordained into the Church of England ministry when he got the surprise of his life. A message in tongues[1] was given during a home meeting which Ralph Goldenberg immediately recognised as Sudanese Arabic.

Having grown up in Sudan with the ability to speak several languages, he knew exactly what it meant. And it could not have been a clearer confirmation of his calling. *"Allah be'hebak – Inta min al dam beta Ibrahiem – Al Angiel fi fomak"* translates as: *"God loves you. You are from the blood of Abraham. The gospel is in your mouth."*

The messenger, who had been unaware that he had spoken in a foreign language which was known and spoken by others, subsequently interpreted what he had said (as instructed by the Apostle Paul in 1 Corinthians 14.27) as: "You are to proclaim the gospel and bring my people to the kingdom."

As recorded in his autobiography, *Find the Truth and Lock it in Your Heart* (www.creativebooksolutions.com), that miraculous incident sparked the beginning of a very fruitful 20-year ministry for the Rev Goldenberg, a former optometrist who has since been helping people to see spiritual truths. Now 72 and retired, Ralph led churches in various parts of England, including the Jewish community of Edgware in north London, where he encountered opposition as well as interest. At his first church, in his home town of Bournemouth, he witnessed the miraculous healing of a missionary to China who had come home for back surgery which was cancelled after prayer and anointing with oil.

The Holy Spirit, who had so empowered the first believers on the Day of Pentecost that they spoke in the languages of Jews from many nations who were staying in Jerusalem for the festival (also known as Shavuot),[2] has clearly played an essential role in Ralph's ministry. He recalls the time when, during a Pentecost Sunday service, "nearly everyone received the Holy Spirit and children spontaneously started praying and prophesying over the adults". His final Pentecost service turned into an impromptu full immersion baptism and lasted four hours.

Ralph was among 40 grandchildren to a Chief Rabbi sent to lead the Jewish community in Sudan, and both his grandparents told him to "Find the truth and lock it in your heart" – hence the book's title. So imagine his surprise when the vicar in charge of the church[3] where he was married a golden 50 years ago (on July 29, 2017) told him to "search for the truth and follow wherever it leads you".

Ralph was sent to a Jewish school in Brighton, England – and seemed to meet Christians at every turn of his life from this point on. He had also, in fact, attended a Catholic school in Sudan. He followed his father into optometry, meeting his wife Helen at the City University in London where she was also an optometry student, and, when he joined an optician's partnership, he too was a Christian!

Ralph and Helen had three lovely boys, a beautiful home and in time seemed to have everything, but still felt empty inside. They joined the Round Table, made friends with a Christian couple and soon became connected with St Mary's, Ferndown. "I am a Jew but I want to know about Jesus," Ralph told the vicar. Helen meanwhile had already been persuaded that Jesus was knocking on the door of her life just waiting to be invited in (Revelation 3.20) and Ralph was duly challenged to read the New Testament, which he found "mind-blowing".

But he needed to be sure that Jesus was divine. So he challenged God to send at least one person – perhaps even six – to say "Jesus is alive!" He subsequently felt drawn to attend church with Helen, and was blown away when a new song was introduced which repeated the line "Jesus is alive today" several times! He never looked back, and it was ten years later, while experiencing pre-ordination nerves, that he got the knockout confirmation of his calling, in Arabic!

Ralph has certainly found the truth his grandparents encouraged him to seek and is currently part of the leadership of the Church's Ministry among Jewish People (CMJ), an international body dedicated to the spiritual rebirth of Israel.

Notes

[1] A New Testament phenomenon foretold in the Tenach (Old Testament) – see Isaiah 28.11, Acts 2.4, 1 Corinthians 14.21.

[2] Acts 2.4f.

[3] St Anne's Bagshot, in Surrey.

Chapter 16

A Bronze Snake and a Narrow Escape

Meanwhile, despite being impressed by the claims of Christianity at a meeting he attended at school, a teenage pupil didn't think it was for him because he was Jewish. But when the speaker assured him that this was no barrier, Nick Howard committed his life to Christ, and subsequently discovered that key sections of the Old Testament (the Jewish Bible) were "all about Jesus".

The son of former British Conservative Party leader Michael Howard, Nick grew in his faith and is now an Anglican minister in New York, married to Betsy and in the early stages of establishing a new church in Manhattan, where up to 20 per cent of the population is Jewish. Nick's background was in liberal Judaism and as such did not involve regular synagogue attendance or strict observance of food laws. But he was proud of his Jewish heritage and had his bar mitzvah 'coming-of-age' ceremony when he turned 13.

"I was very conscious of the suffering experienced by my family during the Holocaust – my great-grandmother was murdered at Auschwitz...," he recalls. However, it didn't give him the answers to life's biggest questions, particularly the inevitability of death. "It seemed to make everything I was doing pointless...Why put so much exertion into living when death makes all that striving utterly meaningless?"

Then, at 15, he went along to a meeting organised by a Christian group. "I was eager to hear a new explanation of life that might finally answer my questions." A pastor named

Jonathan Fletcher spoke on a sentence from the Bible: "Just as Moses lifted up the snake in the desert, so the Son of Man must be lifted up, that everyone who believes in him may have eternal life." (See John 3.14f.)

"In other words, when Jesus was lifted up on the cross, he made it possible for people to live forever," Nick understood. "Moses was addressing the problem of a plague of venomous snakes during the wilderness wanderings of the Israelites. God provided the remedy of a bronze snake fixed to a pole so that, whenever someone was bitten, they could simply look at the bronze snake and live. Jonathan explained that our rebellion against God was more serious than a lethal snakebite, but that Jesus was willingly nailed to the cross to solve that problem by taking the punishment for sin that we deserved. All we have to do is 'look and live'. I knew immediately that eternal life would transform everything for me. But one significant matter still had to be addressed. So I said to Jonathan afterwards: 'I'm Jewish, so I suppose this isn't for me'. But he replied: 'Jesus himself was Jewish! He's the Jewish Messiah – the one the Jews were waiting for down the centuries. If you follow him, you'll be following your own Messiah.'"

Nick was greatly reassured to hear that he could believe in Jesus and still be Jewish. "So I began following Jesus that evening and gratefully received the gift of eternal life." But it was not until his third year of following Jesus that lifestyle changes started to kick in after he saw the need for Christ to be Lord of his life.

"Jesus said: 'Whoever loses his life for me and for the gospel will save it.' (Mark 8.35) It meant the loss of my right to live life my way – like getting drunk with my friends. But if living for Jesus required major changes to my life, I didn't want to implement them without being convinced that he really *was* the promised Messiah. I desperately wanted

Christianity to be true, but that wasn't enough. It had to be *the truth* before I was willing to live it out.

"When my indecision was at its height, I suddenly remembered a talk I'd heard at school on the evidence for the resurrection of Jesus from the dead: the empty tomb with the absent body no-one could account for, and the appearances Jesus made after his death, which had the effect of turning devastated followers into joyful standard-bearers for the faith. I knew I had been thoroughly convinced, at the time of hearing that talk, that the evidence demonstrated that Jesus did indeed rise from the dead, and it was this that persuaded me to remain on 'the narrow road that leads to life' (Matthew 7.14) whatever the consequences."

When Nick read Isaiah chapter 53, he was amazed to discover it was all about Jesus. A friend of his, who is also a Jewish believer, likes to say that Jesus fits the Old Testament prophecies about the Messiah like a finger fits its own fingerprint. "In the light of all this, you might well ask why so few Jews believe in Jesus. One answer is the sad history of persecution by Christians, and another is because so few have heard that it is possible."

Isaiah 52.7 says: "How beautiful on the mountains are the feet of those who bring good news… who say to Zion, 'Your God reigns!'" We need more Jonathans in the world, Nick concludes. "May God raise up many others like him to tell Jewish people throughout the world to look with faith at Jesus, their Messiah, and live forever."[1]

Jewish boy's narrow escape from the Nazis

Snatched from the jaws of the Nazis in the nick of time, Heini Fiege escaped to England to begin a new life. It was a traumatic parting for Heini and his brother Arthur, aged seven and ten at the time, but their parents could see the writing on the wall and willingly gave up their boys for adoption to save them from the horrors of Auschwitz, where they were to perish within a few short years.

Heini and Arthur thus became beneficiaries in 1938 of the *Kindertransport* project of Sir Nicholas Winton, who died recently aged 106. A young stockbroker at the time, he arranged the rescue of 669 Jewish children from Czechoslovakia and other places under German occupation. Despite the heartbreak, which affected him for much of his life, Heini and his brother found new hope as they grew up in Sheffield comforted by the love and devotion of a Christian couple, Les and Vera Cumpston, and their son John.

Shortly after their arrival in Sheffield, foster father Les became the butt of neighbourhood jokes as he set about building an elaborate air-raid shelter in the garden of their home in the southern suburb of Handsworth. But of course, like Noah building an ark on dry ground, he was thoroughly vindicated when the city was heavily blitzed by the Luftwaffe on the nights of 12th and 15th December 1940. Les was under-manager of Tinsley Park Colliery at the time and later moved to nearby Worksop following promotion to Inspector of Mines and Quarries for Nottinghamshire, Derbyshire and South Yorkshire.

Following the lead of his older brother, Heini anglicised his name to John Fieldsend, preferring the English equivalent of his second name Hans. Not surprisingly perhaps in view of his parents' example, John also discovered a personal faith in Christ and, although he qualified as an engineer with practical experience of working on aircraft during his time in the Royal Air Force, he felt a strong call to preach the gospel full-time and became a successful Anglican vicar overseeing a thriving church in Bayston Hill, Shropshire.

Dwelling on his past was difficult to face at first, but in time he felt drawn to re-focus on his Jewish roots, referring to himself as a Messianic Jew – one who follows Jesus as

Messiah. He later became involved in the leadership of CMJ. The Jewish aspect of his identity had taken a leap forward when TV personality Esther Rantzen arranged an emotional 50th anniversary reunion between Sir Nicholas Winton and some of the children he rescued as part of her very popular *That's Life!* programme. Sir Nicholas had kept forged copies of the children's identity documents (forged to speed up the process of officialdom for what he knew to be a dire emergency). These were used to track down the likes of John, who had lost most of his relatives in the Holocaust.

We have already seen how, as recorded in his recently published book *A Wondering Jew* (Radec Press), John realized how close he had come to being among the one-and-a-half million children who died at the hands of the Nazis. His ministry has taken him all over Britain and to many parts of the world, and on one occasion in South Africa, after sharing his story and speaking about Jewish and Gentile reconciliation through Jesus, he was approached by a man who "rather hesitantly confessed that he had spent the war years as a member of the Hitler Youth".

"This was not the first time, nor would it be the last, that I had been challenged to practise what I had just preached!"

John and his wife Elizabeth celebrated their golden wedding in 2011. Now well into his 80s, John is a regular speaker at the Holocaust Museum in Laxton, near Newark, in Nottinghamshire.

Note

[1] Much of the narrative on Nick Howard is taken, with his permission, from The Gospel Coalition's account of his story. See their website at www.thegospelcoalition.org

Chapter 17

Flying Hero Falls from a Dizzy Height

Our attitude to the Jews is vital; it affects our lives whether we like it or not. The story of how one of America's greatest heroes was well and truly knocked off his pedestal almost overnight is a salutary lesson both for his and other nations today.

Charles Lindbergh gripped the world with his tremendous skills as an aviator, becoming the first pilot to cross the Atlantic when he flew non-stop from New York to Paris in the summer of 1927 – and that in a one-seater plane with no forward view!

Millions lined the streets of American cities to hail the heroism of this handsome boy from Minnesota; streets and schools were named after him; he was fêted and wooed by politicians. In an age when celebrities were generally confined to the glitz and glamour of the emerging film industry in Hollywood, Lindbergh captured the imagination in a way no one else had managed.

But then, just as America was about to enter World War II, he rose to make a speech urging them to stay out of the conflict. By this time he was a known Nazi sympathiser, being much influenced by the 'science' of eugenics which sought to ensure the continuance of a pure race without physical, mental or other defects. As for Jews, they were partly to blame for the war, along with Britain and America, in his view. In fact, he went on, they were a particularly malign influence because of their ownership and domination of "our motion pictures, our press, our radio, and our government".

The high-flying hero crashed to the ground in the minds of his listeners almost before he had finished his speech, which was being broadcast on national radio. His name came off streets and schools and airports. TWA (Trans World Airlines) stopped calling itself 'the Lindbergh Line'. A 1957 movie about his flight to Paris, starring Jimmy Stewart, was a failure at the box office. As the years passed, he largely withdrew from public life. By taking sides against the Jews, Lindbergh had touched 'the apple of God's eye' and was either ignorant or defiant of the Scriptures – that those who bless the seed of Abraham will themselves be blessed, but those who curse them will come under judgment.

The enigmatic aviator is featured among a host of characters – many of them anti-heroes – in Bill Bryson's best-selling *One Summer – America 1927*, a truly fascinating read with a liberal sprinkling of his trademark humour that also includes a peek at Henry Ford, the car magnate, who might have avoided some of his own troubles – including commercial ones – if he too had not insisted on berating the Jews. He did, however, regret breaking the Sabbath, admitting that his much-heralded Model A would have been ready in half the time had he not made its designers work at weekends and evenings.

Looking at the bigger picture, Britain's rise and fall virtually parallels its actions for and against Israel. By the turn of the 20th century, it was said that the sun never set on its empire, with much of the globe covered in pink in our atlases. We were blessed with great power, authority and influence, and it is my belief that it was entirely due to the consistent way in which Evangelical Christians had prayed for and loved the Jews – because they read in the Scriptures that this is God's will and command – to such an extent that they even prevailed on the Government of the day to do all in its power to provide a homeland for the Jewish people.

As much as we were blessed when true Christianity influenced our politicians, we have come under a terrible curse since successive governments (backed by a sleepy church) sought to appease Arabs rather than look to Israel's best interests. We lost our empire, and we lost our way as a nation which once spread the good news of Jesus, the Jew, all over the world. We have rejected the Judeo-Christian civilisation on which our nation was built, so it is hardly surprising that the social fabric of society is collapsing around our ears. Part of the ongoing problem with the West, especially as it affects Israel, is that the church needs to wake up.

But I must pay tribute to Mike Evans, already mentioned as the man behind the new Friends of Zion Heritage Centre in Jerusalem which seeks to demonstrate that true Christians through the ages have loved and supported the Chosen People – some of them even paying with their lives. These include the Dutch woman Corrie ten Boom, whose family hid Jews from the Nazis. She ended up in the Ravensbrück concentration camp and had to watch her sister dying in the terrible conditions. She later met one of the camp guards, who had become a Christian – and with great difficulty, but with God's help, she managed to forgive him!

A brave Scot's Auschwitz horror

Another such heroine was Scotland's Jane Haining, who died in Auschwitz after being 'convicted' of the crime of loving the Jewish girls in her care at a boarding establishment in Budapest, Hungary, where she was matron. Just six months before the Auschwitz-Birkenau camp was liberated by the Red Army on January 27, 1945, the life of this courageous Christian came to a grisly end in its gas chambers. Seventy years on, her story came into sharp focus with the publication of a new book. It has even been translated into Hungarian, and a key Budapest thoroughfare has been named after her. Yet, in truth, anti-Semitism there is once more on the rise, inflamed by the policies of the right-wing Jobbik Party.

From Matron to Martyr – one woman's ultimate sacrifice for the Jews is authored by New Zealander Lynley Smith, a distant relative who travelled the world to research details for her magnificent portrayal of this brave woman from Dunscore, near Dumfries – the only Scot to be honoured with a 'Righteous Among the Nations' award by Jerusalem's Yad Vashem Holocaust Museum.

Jane had been living and working in the Glasgow area before taking on the role of matron at a school run by the Scottish Mission to Jews. So dedicated was she to what she believed was her life's calling that she refused to leave her post when given several opportunities to escape, and even being ordered home by her superiors who feared for her safety. But more important to her was the safety of the Jewish girls under her care, already suffering under relentless discrimination and persecution even before the Nazis marched into their country. Many of their parents were forcibly split up by the authorities as they sent the breadwinning Jewish men away, ostensibly to work camps, leaving families destitute and distressed.

The children often took refuge in the arms of Jane, who loved to comfort them with hugs and prayers of assurance. When she was forced by new laws to sew yellow stars onto the uniforms of her girls, she sobbed uncontrollably. When some of the poorer pupils had no footwear, she effectively cut off any remaining ties with her homeland by using the soft leather of her suitcase to make soles for the girls' shoes.

Jane was eventually arrested by the Gestapo on a series of charges which basically amounted to the fact that she showed too much concern for the Jews. Leaving her girls distraught, she was moved around various local prisons before being corralled into a cattle truck, crushed in with some 90 other women in conditions worse than animals would suffer, with access neither to water nor toilets for the long and tortuous journey to Auschwitz in south-west Poland.

She died soon afterwards, allegedly of natural causes. But since she had a strong constitution and had held up well even when sharing her food with her fellow inmates in an earlier prison, she is more likely to have been either shot or gassed, like so many of the four million others estimated to have perished at this most infamous of all death camps. A postcard written two days before her death indicated no ill-health, but hinted at her impending 'promotion' to meet with her Lord in heaven. Intriguingly, in a chapter titled *A View from the Summit* early on in the book, the author imagines the scene of Jane's arrival in paradise, which serves the useful purpose of taking the sting out of the horrors that ensue in the narrative. Indeed, the Bible speaks of how the promise of resurrection removes the sting of death.

But little appears to have changed since those dark days in 1944. The author has told me how, on a recent visit to Budapest to launch the Hungarian translation of her book, she witnessed a group of skinheads racing through the city, one of them giving a 'Heil Hitler' salute as he dashed past a policeman. Jobbik lawmaker Marton Gyongyosi sparked protests in 2012 by calling in parliament for a list of people "of Jewish origin (who) present a national security risk to Hungary". Other Jobbik members have referred to the "so-called Holocaust" and have strongly supported the rehabilitation of figures sympathetic to the Nazis like Hungary's wartime leader and Hitler ally Miklos Horthy. Another deputy, Sandor Porzse, has said Hungarians "are the victims of a Jewish conspiracy to colonise our land and rob our resources"; foreign farmers are witnessing increasing incidents of boycott and intimidation from the far right.

Arthur Reynolds, an Englishman who has farmed there since 1991, says: "Hungary has not improved much since 1944."

As I was meditating one day on Psalm 126 – that "those who sow in tears will reap with songs of joy" – I thought of Jane Haining, who wept uncontrollably as she was forced to sew yellow stars on the uniforms of the Jewish girls in her care. A harvest of life from the dead would surely follow, of which the rebirth of Israel was just the beginning. As the Rabbi who wrote a foreword to Lynley's book said, "Jews need to know that true followers of Jesus are our friends."

RECONCILIATION

Chapter 18

Middle East Peace in Manchester

The massacre of the innocents in Manchester, England, on May 22, 2017 – when 22 died and more than a hundred were injured – was a shocking reversal of scenes I witnessed in the city two years earlier which was a perfect picture of reconciliation and peace. The twisted ideology of Islamist suicide bomber Salman Abedi was a complete contrast to the loving arms I saw reaching out to one another when delegates from all over the Arab world came together for a unique conference. As Iran continued its aggressive stance against Israel, threatening to wipe the Jewish state off the map, Iranian refugees and asylum seekers now living in Britain embraced their Jewish 'brothers', some of whom had travelled from Jerusalem to meet them. Also present was a sizeable contingent of Egyptians, along with representatives from Sudan, Saudi Arabia, Jordan, Turkey, Iraq, Lebanon and Algeria. Others wanting to join them had been unable to get visas.

As part of the great untold story of the Middle East, the three-day conference was hosted by CMJ. Although working mainly among Jews since its founding in 1809, CMJ have also consistently been reaching out to Arabs over the years and, in 2012, held their first *At the Crossroads* conference at their Jerusalem headquarters to enable Jew and Gentile to express their oneness in Christ and work together to spread the gospel on the basis of a prophecy from Isaiah (chapter

19) of a "highway" of peace and reconciliation from Egypt to Assyria (which includes much of the modern-day Arab world) via Israel.

For the second of what is now a bi-annual event, in 2014 (covered in my book *Peace in Jerusalem*, available from olivepresspublisher.com), a number of UK-based Iranians, as well as a group of Egyptians, were turned back at the border and thus missed out on a chance to meet up with other Muslim-background believers from all over the region at a conference hosted by Jewish believers in Jesus, generally known as Messianic Jews. And so, *UK at the Crossroads* was arranged to encourage and inspire those who would struggle – mainly due to visa issues – to enter Israel.

David Friedman, a Messianic rabbi from Jerusalem, was delighted that so many Iranians had turned up for the conference – they have established thriving churches throughout England – and implored them to join him in praying for barriers to be broken between their two countries. "We need to get together and pray for our two nations," he said. Before he had finished speaking, they came forward to pray for him, and for Israel! It was an awesome moment – something akin to an earthquake in reverse as a shattered and broken world is put back together again, with all the pieces mended.

Sessions were interspersed with times of worship in Arabic, Farsi (the language spoken in Iran), Hebrew and English, creating a beautiful atmosphere of shared love and identity. Communication may have been a challenge at times, but you only had to look into each other's eyes to know you were one in Christ who, in the words of St Paul, destroys the dividing wall of hostility, creating "one new man" out of the two, thus making peace and reconciling both of them to God through the cross. (See Ephesians 2.14-16.)

One Egyptian musician was playing a lute, a modern

version of the ancient instrument played 3,000 years ago by Israel's King David. Prayer was also offered in various languages with translators on hand for some of the speakers. Beirut-based Robert Sakr, one of the visionaries behind the conference, said: "There's no such thing as a peace process apart from Jesus. In the 55 years I've lived in the Middle East, there has been no political solution."

It was ironic, in light of the current enmity between Iran and Israel, that when the 1967 Six-Day War broke out, his family fled to Iran for safety. But the Islamic Revolution of 1979 had changed all that.

Iranians pray for Jewish rabbi

David Friedman, who is descended from Kings David and Solomon, reminded the Iranian delegates of a time in ancient days when a Persian king (Cyrus) opened the door for his people to come back home, and he prayed that God would so pour out his Spirit that hatred of Israel (among the authorities) would be melted by love. The alternative was a nuclear conflagration that would destroy not only the Middle East, but possibly the entire world.

David's father was a Nazi hunter much pained by witnessing the effects of the Holocaust, but his mother encouraged him to pray. Then his best friend became a believer in Jesus. "I saw that someone was giving him the courage to face his problems," he recalls. "I asked God to reveal himself to me, and the next thing was that I knew… I just knew… that Yeshua was the Messiah."

But he became troubled by the reality of living in a nation always at war with its neighbours – he and his wife personally experienced two terror attacks. He was thus drawn by the promise of the road to reconciliation described by Isaiah (19.23-25) and became involved with others in seeking fellowship and mutual co-operation with Arab brothers, giving hope "in the great sea of hopelessness that engulfs every nation in the Middle East".

Key figures behind the vision of working towards a fulfilment of the 'Isaiah 19 Highway' are Robert Sakr and Michael Kerem, along with Rev David Pileggi, Rector of Christ Church in Jerusalem, built in 1849 by CMJ. The reconciliation for which they have such a passion is reflected in the marriages of both Robert and Michael. Robert was brought up in Tel Aviv and his wife, Miriam, was raised among the Arab people of Jordan. Their current focus is a fulfilment of a word they received from a Dutchwoman at a discipleship conference in Cyprus back in 1978 that, in representing the two countries, they would become a blessing to the surrounding nations. Michael, on the other hand, is a Jew who met his Armenian wife Alis in Turkey.

The Isaiah 19 Highway, from Assyria to Egypt via Israel, represents the very path travelled by Abraham, father of the Jewish race, and so it is perfectly appropriate that it is also the road to peace for Isaac and Ishmael, the sons of Abraham.

Rev Pileggi, meanwhile, comes from an Italian background, and moved to Jerusalem from the United States nearly 40 years ago. He said: "Understanding Jesus in his Jewish context has made all the difference for our faith. For Jesus, in most cases, reference to the kingdom of heaven was about the here and now, not the hereafter. And Isaiah 19 is a very practical way to extend God's kingdom in a region that's controlled by the devil."

Meanwhile, Michael Kerem expressed his sorrow to the Iranians for the unforeseen problems that led to the deportation of most of their contingent travelling to the previous year's conference in Jerusalem. They were interrogated for 48 hours at Tel Aviv's Ben Gurion Airport before being deported on the basis that they represented an element of risk despite holding British passports. But the positive outcome of this is that the Israeli authorities apparently now understand how much Muslim-background believers in Jesus want to visit the country of his birth and ministry, where he died and was raised from the dead, and to which he is returning.

"They also want to come to Israel to meet their Jewish brothers, which could mean that God is going to use 'Ishmael' to open the eyes of 'Isaac' (referring to the mass recognition of Christ as their Messiah prophesied in the Scriptures)", Michael added.

Turkish Christians apologise for Armenian genocide

The conference also heard how Turkish Christians recently met with a group of Armenians to apologise for the genocide that took place 100 years ago. Admitting a mistake goes very much against the grain in the Middle East, but they embraced in the name of Jesus and a Turkish pastor, Ali Pektash, got down on his knees to wash the feet of an elderly Armenian, apologising for what his grandparents had done, whereupon the Armenian responded by washing the feet of his Turkish brother-in-Christ.

"Forgive me for what my people have done in killing, torturing and forcefully converting and expelling you from our land," Ali told his hosts, asking them to pray that the curse he believed had come upon his nation as a result would be lifted. The Armenians, along with a group of Yazidi Kurds, duly prayed for their visitors and forgave them. And when two pastors who had been at loggerheads with each other saw what happened, it melted their hearts and they were reconciled.

Robert Sakr frankly admitted that he did not understand what was happening in the Middle East today with borders being wiped out and bloodshed on a horrific scale. "But I know that God is in control and that the harvest will come in an environment of both persecution and blessing," he said.

Referring to Jesus' parable of the weeds (Matthew 13) in which he explains that the weeds, planted by an enemy, should be left to grow with the wheat until the harvest, Robert said that while organisations like CNN and the BBC were focused on covering news about the weeds, "we must take care of news about the wheat – we're the 'good news' people; our job is telling people what God is doing, not the enemy."

He said that although Zionism and Arab aspirations are incompatible, God has the last word. For 67 years some of the smartest people in the world have tried to solve this problem. It's a puzzle. But I'm focusing on the crop of wheat which is growing and expanding. Israel was a spiritual desert when I was growing up. Now there are so many believers. We need to focus on the wheat."

Iranian says, "I love Israel"

One Iranian delegate made the astonishing declaration: "I may be from Iran, but I love Israel, and there are Christians praying for Israel inside Iran."

A refugee forced to flee Iran because he had become a Christian and whose name is being withheld for security reasons, the young man spoke of the growing church in his adopted city led by a pastor who gives clear teaching about the special place of Israel in God's purposes. With the government and police on his case after converting from Islam (which is against the law), he and his wife fled Iran several years ago, hidden in a wooden box on the back of a lorry for a tortuous 72-day journey to the UK. God watched over every detail, even in directing him to an Iranian church when he finally arrived in an English city.

Although financially secure in Iran with a house and car, he was empty inside and became disillusioned by the harshness of Islam. A troubled home life did not help and he became addicted to medicinal drugs until he learnt to play the sitar when, for the first time in his life, he was given a hug and began to share his problems with his tutor who eventually prayed for him with the laying on of hands in Jesus' name. He was instantly healed, and subsequently became a believer. Now he wakes up every morning thanking Jesus for bringing him out of darkness.

Another ex-Muslim from Iran struggled to comprehend the harshness of the religion and was "switched on" to Christianity after watching a film about Jesus. She initially came to the UK to visit relatives and subsequently married an Englishman. Her faith, however, was put on the back burner until her five-week-old daughter was diagnosed with a tumour. It reminded her that she was a Christian who "knew someone who could sort it out" and her little girl recovered so well that she was even swimming by the age of five.

A teenage boy, born in Tehran, told the conference how he turned his back on strict Muslim observance when his heart was touched by a church's worship band. Music was regarded as sinful among his radical group. But he was sickened by the brutal treatment of soldiers and shocked by the discovery of guns in a mosque. He realised he was being taught to kill and control people. He had been reaching out to God from an early age, but had found no answers until – in the UK – he heard people talking of Jesus. He reluctantly accepted an invitation to church, where his heart was melted by the music. As he put it, "They told me this wasn't about religion, but a relationship with God, which was exactly what I had been looking for all those years. I gave my heart to Jesus Christ, and what a difference it made. Now he's my Lord, my God …my everything!"

An Iranian bishop, meanwhile, spoke of the suffering endured by Christians in a country where he also experienced discrimination as a member of the Jewish community, who were forced to live in designated areas. Rt Rev Iraj Kalimi Mottahedh came to faith in Jesus through the influence of his uncle and became minister of a church visited by the Queen and the Shah of Iran. But when the revolution struck in 1979, the Anglican Church was the first to be targeted. A pastor was killed and an assassination attempt was made on the then bishop. Iraj then took charge when the bishop left, but was imprisoned for eight months, unable to leave the country for twelve years and forbidden to accept Muslim converts into his church.

A young refugee from Saudi Arabia told the conference how he became a Christian through listening to a radio broadcast. Now he prays that God will birth a church in his home country, where conversion from Islam is strictly forbidden. As he put it, "I'm different now. I feel optimistic, and I have hope." Referring to Christians, he said: "These people are the hope of this earth and the solution for its troubles."

A Jordanian believer working among refugees in strife-torn Iraq said that, amidst all the mayhem created by the ruthless Islamic State terrorists, many Yazidis and others are turning to Christ. He has been able to distribute Bibles among soldiers and government officials.

A young woman from Algeria, where a revival of Christianity is reported to be taking place, spoke of the joy she found when she accepted Jesus into her life. Although growing up as a devoted Muslim with a love for God, she had a lot of questions and became convinced by the truth and reality of Christ as the Son of God after tuning in to a Christian TV channel. She said, "I accepted Jesus as my Saviour, although I had great difficulty with the concept of him being the Son of God, but it soon became clear to me that he was. I was full of joy and the love of God was within me. I wanted to hug everybody and forgive those who opposed me. I talked with everybody about Jesus." But she paid a price for her faith, suffering opposition from her brother and losing a good job with the United Nations. She said, "Despite this I have a great experience with the Lord, who provides me with everything I need, and I want to dedicate my life completely to serving him."

Chapter 19

Muslim Pilgrim Finds Jesus in Mecca

Among those testifying at the Manchester conference was a former Muslim from Turkey who went on a pilgrimage to Mecca in a desperate bid to get his life straightened out – and met Jesus! A wife-beater who was addicted to alcohol, Ali Pektash was on a visit to the famous shrine when he fell asleep in the oppressive heat. Jesus twice appeared to him in a dream, telling him to leave the area and spread the gospel, and left a permanent mark where he touched him on the chest.

One of ten children in a family of Kurds, he was rejected by his mother, which opened a deep wound in his life. He was taken in by his uncle, but he too chased him out. At 14 he ran away to work in the construction industry before returning home four years later at the invitation of his father.

The communists were gaining influence in his region, but when he started work as a shepherd he could not understand how people could curse God whose beautiful creation he witnessed in the fields every day. He met and married Zehra (who accompanied him to the conference), but said he was a weak-willed man who succumbed to heavy drinking which began to destroy his life. He would start to shake if he did not have a drink and things got so bad that he was beating his wife several times a day and struggling to breathe after just a few steps.

Friends persuaded him to find work in Saudi Arabia, where he could get free of alcohol because it was forbidden. But in fact he was to discover there was plenty of it available there. Perhaps Mecca held the key to success, they suggested, so he agreed to join a group on hajj (pilgrimage) during his time in Arabia.

Speaking through an interpreter, he said: "I knew I belonged to God somehow – he was my friend – but I did not belong to a religion I could find. I circled the Ka'ba (the cube-like building at the centre of the Great Mosque) seven times (one of the specified rites involved in the pilgrimage), and watched everybody kissing this black stone. But I walked the other way. I believed in a living God, not in a rock."

When they retreated to their tents for the night, he chose to sleep under the stars because it was so hot. "Jesus came to me in a dream, put his finger on my forehead and his hand on my heart. He was smiling at me and said: 'Get up and leave this place'. I didn't really understand, but I knew I was saved. There was a vibration in my kidney area where it felt like someone was speaking to me, and he kept saying the same thing. I became very afraid, and remembered reading how too much alcohol could affect your brain. I thought maybe I was going crazy; that my end had come. I told my friends what had happened, but they laughed it off, saying I had eaten too much, and they asked: 'What does Jesus have to do with Mohammed?'

"But the voice would not leave me alone. I told my friends I couldn't finish the hajj, but they got upset and angry. I found a bathroom where I took a shower before I left and saw in a mirror that the black hair on my chest had the white imprint of a hand on one side. I tried to rub it off, thinking it might be dust, and heard the voice say, 'You're going to see a lot more things than this.' So I got down on my knees and said, 'Lord, whatever you want from me I will do.' He told me that I should go directly back home, so I immediately left the construction company for whom I had been working."

He rang his wife to say he was coming home with Jesus, which naturally puzzled her as she was looking around to see where his companion was when he landed. "He's inside me," he explained. In accordance with tradition for those who return from hajj, neighbours all turned out for a welcome home party. "I obeyed the Lord's instruction by standing up and telling everyone present that I had become a Christian. Some got upset and left the room. That night I told Zehra that I couldn't live with her anymore because I was a Christian and she was a Muslim."

But she responded: "Whatever you want to be, I'll become."

Although Ali knew he was now a Christian and passionately shared his testimony with others, it was six long years before he was able to obtain a Bible in his own language – through a Christian radio station in Russia. "It was the most precious gift I received in my entire life. I read it all before I ate or slept again," he said. "I memorised whole portions and this book changed my life. I kept reading it over and over, understanding more as I did so."

God's word also brought healing to his life, curing his addiction to drink and cigarettes, along with his wife-beating antics.

It was another year before he met his first Christian compatriot (apart from his wife) – a pastor in Istanbul. He studied there and became a pastor himself in Ankara, the capital. Now his goal is to see a believer in every Turkish home, and his hope is that they will then help fulfil Isaiah's vision of a highway of reconciliation from Egypt to Assyria via Israel.

Jesus is still Jewish – Rector

Addressing the conference on the Hebraic roots of the Christian faith, Rev Pileggi said: "If we don't understand Jesus in his Jewish context, we will fail to see him fully as he really is. Jesus is a Jew who still keeps his identity. He is described in Revelation (the last book of the Bible) as the 'Root of David' and the 'Lion of the tribe of Judah' and still identifies with the Jewish people. While it's perfectly possible to be a Christian and not know about the Jewishness of Jesus, such knowledge brings added blessing and helps us to be better disciples. It gives us a better understanding of his sayings, which in turn will help us develop a more intimate relationship with him."

Adding that Judaism is often mischaracterised as legalism, he pointed out that the New Testament has over 1,000 commandments. "God is first of all the God of Israel who has revealed himself first to Abraham, Isaac and Jacob, and the New Covenant is given to the people of Israel and Judah. The Jewish people are called to be priests in order to serve the nations. They have done great things (such as producing Nobel prize-winners out of all proportion to their numbers) because God is great. We worship the God of the Jews. The Apostle Paul recognised the great spiritual debt we owe the Jews by his concern for their poor. But we're not talking about approving everything the state of Israel does."

A tidal wave of secular culture has swept over the West, he added, but Jews had preserved the culture of the Bible – singing, praying and even eating it, as it were, referring to their many feasts based on biblical events. "Their faith is their culture – the sanctity of the Sabbath, for example, and the religious holidays (holy-days). And all of us should stand up against anti-Semitism, praying for Israel to live out God's calling."

The Complete Picture!

Jesus completed the picture of her life for Hazel Williams, a Jewish woman from Bristol, whose Austrian parents sought refuge from the Nazis here in 1938. And she identified with the many other refugees at the conference. For years she was embarrassed about her Jewish identity due to the anti-Semitism that had forced her family to leave Austria, but she has since developed a growing love for her people. She became a Christian at a time when she felt very alone following divorce. It was Good Friday 1982 when she heard a voice saying that she would never again be alone. "I knew it was Jesus," she said. "And from that day I was a believer. I now know I am complete."

Chapter 20

A Modern Damascus Road Conversion

Back in Israel, meanwhile, the amazing story of Mosab Hassan Yousef is further proof of the point made by our Manchester conference delegates – that peace is possible through Jesus. Son of the founder of terror group Hamas, committed to the destruction of Israel, Mosab grew up causing trouble in the West Bank and later switched sides after being sickened by the hypocrisy and deceit he witnessed.

"There is hope for peace in the Middle East, but it does not begin with political solutions or negotiations; it begins with the changing of individual hearts," he writes in a new edition of his New York Times bestseller, *Son of Hamas*. His story is now also told in *The Green Prince*, an award-winning documentary.

Mosab was just 18 when he was first arrested by the Israelis who found him in possession of weapons (that turned out not to work). After being severely beaten up during interrogation, he succumbed to the lure of being a collaborator. Although hating the Jews, he persuaded himself that he was a 'double agent' with the ultimate intention of killing his new masters. But as he witnessed fellow inmates being tortured by their Muslim 'brothers' on the flimsiest evidence of being informers, he was increasingly nauseated by the insincerity of those among whom he mixed, both in and out of jail. They pretended their cause was for the love of their people, but in reality cared little for anything but lining their own pockets and giving full expression to their hatred of the 'enemy'.

Ironically, his famous father was a loving family man caught up in political intrigue he did not fully understand. At the same time, Mosab was developing a close friendship with his contact for Shin Bet, the Israeli secret service, whose kindness was in sharp contrast to the brutal dealings of his Muslim colleagues. Mosab ended up working for Shin Bet for ten years – with the codename *Green Prince* (as heir apparent to the green-flagged Hamas) – during which time he witnessed many gruesome scenes, including the aftermath of suicide bombings and the bloodbath often ensuing from a clash between the IDF (Israeli Defence Force) and some of those he 'shopped'. Though at constant risk to his own life, he became a vital cog in Israel's spy network and there is no doubt that many innocent lives were saved as a result.

In the midst of these shadowy activities, he had a literal 'Damascus Road' experience. He was walking past the imposing Damascus Gate leading into Jerusalem's Old City when he was invited to a Bible study at the YMCA where he was introduced to the New Testament, and to Jesus. He was powerfully impacted by the words of Jesus – especially his 'Sermon on the Mount' and his call to "love your enemies" – which greatly affected his ongoing surveillance work; at times he even managed to persuade his bosses simply to arrest, rather than assassinate, dangerous men suspected of plotting mass murder.

He eventually broke away entirely from his Islamic roots and fully embraced Jesus as the Son of God. But his full, amazing story could not be told until he was safely in America, where the courts initially wanted to send him back – to almost certain death – because they would not believe his testimony. Following his conscience, and his faith, has cost him dearly – his family, to whom he is devoted, have disowned him. Such is the price many with Mosab's Muslim background have had to pay as disciples of Jesus. Published by Tyndale Momentum, *Son of Hamas* was co-authored by Ron Brackin and includes a new chapter on his U.S. court hearing.

The costly path of discipleship in Israel

Further insight into the reconciliation taking place in Israel is beautifully told in a spell-binding new book by British journalist and broadcaster Julia Fisher. *What is God doing in Israel?* (published by Monarch) is a gripping account of the lives of individual Jews and Arabs who have had a supernatural encounter with Jesus. In each case it has led to a dramatic transformation in their lives. The cost of their discipleship – whether coming from a Jewish or Muslim background – has been no less demanding than that experienced by St Paul and the original apostles. For there is nothing half-hearted about their faith, with passion undimmed despite painful suffering, especially through rejection by family or community.

Appropriately, the book is divided into twelve chapters. Most of the Jewish believers included have been disowned by their families at some point – in the case of Sandy Shoshani it was 14 years before she was reconciled with her father, who subsequently gave his life to Jesus on his deathbed. As Jesus said: "No-one who has left home or brothers or sisters or mother or father or children or fields for me and the gospel will fail to receive a hundred times as much in this present age (homes, brothers, sisters, mothers, children and fields – and with them, persecutions) and in the age to come, eternal life" (Mark 10.29).

Also featured is the more widely-known story of David and Leah Ortiz, whose teenage son Ami was virtually blown apart by a bomb (though he has since miraculously recovered). Perversely disguised as a Purim parcel, the device was sent to the family home during the Feast of Purim, when Jews exchange gifts to celebrate their rescue, by Queen Esther, from a plot to exterminate them in ancient times. The perpetrator of the atrocity, a Jewish extremist, believed the Ortiz family were betraying his people by encouraging them to follow Jesus.

As far as some of the Muslim-background believers are concerned, they have become like hunted animals after deciding to follow Christ, with Julia having to carry out interviews with a great degree of stealth and care so as not to attract attention to these brave men and women risking their lives for the sake of their Lord. Many have been tortured, imprisoned or forced to flee the land.

The shocking irony of it all is that these persecuted believers actually hold the key to peace in this troubled region. Palestinian and Jewish believers are clearly united by their love for Yeshua, the Jewish Messiah; they pray and have fellowship with one another and are a powerful demonstration of the reconciling effect of what Jesus did for them on the cross, breaking down the dividing wall of hostility and creating "one new man" out of the two (see Ephesians 2.14). "This is something the politicians cannot do," said Mazen Naswari, a Palestinian pastor in Jerusalem's Old City. "This love that we as believers in Jesus share, no matter what background we come from, shows that we can love one another."

Patrick Radecker was a seemingly hopeless drug addict who lived on the streets for seven years but, with the help of a rehabilitation centre in Haifa called House of Victory, he has been totally cleaned up and renewed, almost unrecognisable to those with whom he used to hang out in downtown Tel Aviv. A Jew whose family immigrated to Israel from Holland,

Patrick too has developed a special love for Arabs since he started following Yeshua.

Here is the answer to conflict in the Middle East – all these people, Jews and Arabs, have found peace through the Messiah whom the prophet Isaiah foretold would be the 'Prince of Peace' (see Isaiah 9.6). In fact, I see Julia's book as a divine romance, for it tells the wondrous story of how falling in love with Jesus brings former enemies together so that the sons of Isaac embrace the sons of Ishmael.

Julia's own charity, the Olive Tree Reconciliation Fund (www.olivetreefund.org), builds bridges across the political and social divide by helping suffering families in a practical way.

REPENTANCE

Chapter 21

Britain's Broken Pledge

We have seen how, after doing so much to promote the restoration of Israel in the century leading up to the Balfour Declaration, Britain subsequently moved in precisely the opposite direction. Its continued policy of appeasing the Arabs most likely led to the death of hundreds of thousands, if not millions, of Jews who could have escaped Hitler's concentration camps through emigration to Palestine. While restricting Jewish immigration, they simultaneously failed to regulate Arab immigration. Even after the war, hundreds of thousands of Holocaust survivors were denied their right to return to their own land at a time when they had nowhere else to go, thus contravening the purpose for which it had been established. In addition, post-war Britain went out of its way to ensure the new state would not survive, even appointing a British officer, Lt Gen Sir John Bagot Glubb, to command the Jordanian Arab Legion. British military support for the appointment of Haj Amin al-Husseini as Grand Mufti of Jerusalem gave fundamentalist Islam a foothold in the Lord's Land, leaving the anti-Jewish legacy that persists to this day. Justice for Jews, meanwhile, was scant; following the massacre at Hebron, for example, Britain uprooted the entire Jewish community there – the oldest in the world.

Moreover, newly-released documents reveal that only one in four Jewish victims of the Nazis who applied for compensation from a British fund were paid. Of the 4,206 applicants for remunerative reparation from the so-called Nazi Persecution Compensation fund given to Britain by Germany in 1964, only 1,015 received any money. In documents made public by the British Government's National Archives, it emerges that those who requested compensation were subject to intense and insensitive questioning and nit-picking, and the majority were ultimately rejected.

In her disobedience to God long ago, Israel was sold into the hands of her enemies (Judges 2.14), and it appears that Britain is suffering the same fate today. We own few of our major industries or football clubs, for one thing; we have had a justice system effectively run by Europe (which will hopefully change following the Brexit vote), and have presided over a steep decline in churchgoing while Islam – the antithesis of Christianity in so many ways, particularly as regards freedom – has established a strong foothold in the nation.

In a message given just three months before his death in 2003, Derek Prince saw "very little hope for Britain". Repeating his warning that "the nation not serving Israel would perish" (Isaiah 60.12), he said that, although he did not live in the UK, his impression was that few Christians there were being raised to warn the British people about their attitude to Israel. "Few nations have been so favoured by God as the British... but right now we are on top of a slippery slope, which will lead us to disaster."

Persecutors of Jews queue up to say sorry!

Fortunately, amidst rising anti-Semitism, there appears to be a somewhat surprising parallel move towards repentance by some European nations for the many shameful actions taken against Jews over the centuries.

The latest comes from Spain who, having expelled some 300,000 Jews in 1492, have now invited their descendants back! The Sephardic Ancestry Act aims to correct an "historic mistake" by offering citizenship to as many as 3.5 million Sephardic Jews around the world whose ancestors were forced out by King Ferdinand and Queen Isabella.[1] Neighbouring Portugal has in recent years passed a similar 'Law of Return' offering citizenship to the many Sephardic Jews they persecuted, including my own ancestors. So I guess that entitles me to Portuguese citizenship!

These are welcome moves which contrast sharply with the growing hostility towards Jewish communities being demonstrated in Europe generally, not only in the desecration of synagogues and personal attacks but in the calls for boycotts and condemnation in the political and economic sphere. No doubt Spain has been influenced by their former Prime Minister Jose Maria Aznar who, in a *Times* article some years ago, urged support for Israel on the basis that "if it goes down, we all go down".[2] He argued that the Jewish state is at the cutting edge of the battle between militant Islam and the West and concluded: "Israel is a fundamental part of the West which is what it is thanks to its Judeo-Christian roots. If the Jewish element of those roots is upturned and Israel lost, then we are lost too. Whether we like it or not our fate is inextricably intertwined."

And in 2008 a Spanish newspaper is said to have published a hard-hitting article expressing similar sentiments – regretting the part Europe had played in an attempt to destroy a people who had pursued nothing but life and peace while at the same time welcoming Muslims whose extremist ranks blew up trains and hijacked planes. It does at least continue to demonstrate the potential power for good inherent in the printed word in a world where there is an ever-intensifying battle between truth and propaganda.

Meanwhile a group of nearly 200 British Christians took part in a day of repentance at the port of Haifa in Israel to apologise and make amends for the way in which their government turned back Jewish refugees fleeing war-torn Europe 70 years ago, preventing tens of thousands from landing in their biblical homeland apparently because they exceeded a quota on immigration.

Despite being perfectly placed for fulfilling their pledge to assist with the creation of a Jewish homeland, Britain prevented more than 90 ships from landing at Haifa between 1938 and 1948, according to Julie Stahl and Chris Mitchell in an article for CBN News. And Col Richard Kemp, former commander of British forces in Afghanistan, is reported as saying: "I'm here to commemorate those Jews…who suffered or died as a result of the shameful policies of the British government of the day."[3]

Rosie Ross, who organised the day, said: "We turned them away and put them in camps in Cyprus and Mauritius, and some were even returned to deportation camps in Germany." Others were locked up in a detention camp in Atlit, south of Haifa.

Lord Simon Isaacs, speaking at the event, said the quota on immigration breached Britain's contract with the Jewish people ratified at the treaties of San Remo (1920) and Versailles (1923). He said there were two reasons behind their behaviour: appeasing the Arabs and a Labour government that was essentially anti-Jewish.

Notes

[1] Shira Rubin, *newrepublic.com*, May 20 2015 http://www.newrepublic.com/article/121865/spains-passport-offer-sephardic-jews-raises-debate-israel?utm_source=Sailthru&utm_medium=email&utm_term=TNR%20Daily%20Newsletter&utm_campaign=Daily%20Newsletter%20-%205%2F21%2F15

[2] Jose Maria Aznar, *The Times*, June 17 2010.

[3] Julie Stahl and Chris Mitchell, *CBN News*, June 5 2015.

BATTLES AHEAD

Chapter 22

A Nuclear War of Words

As the world shudders at talk of a possible nuclear war, it is worth pointing out that the real confrontation is, as ever, a spiritual one. As the battle between light and darkness rages on, a high-tech media with global reach has the potential to influence as never before. But in this brave new upside-down world, truth is so often turned on its head.

The horrific Paris massacre naturally focused media attention, yet there has been relatively little coverage of the almost daily terror in Israel where Palestinian perpetrators have been portrayed as underdogs with a just cause while the real victims of these unprovoked stabbing and shooting attacks were innocent Jews. It is not about allegedly stolen land or oppressive occupation; it is sheer hatred of Jews that is behind every attack, with social and other media fanning the flames of incitement. PA president Mahmoud Abbas calls on the UN to "protect Palestinians from Israeli aggression" while at the same time calling on Palestinians to take up knives against Israelis.[1]

Two teenage Palestinian girls viciously attacked a 70-year-old man with scissors right beside a bustling open-air market in Jerusalem. And yet the victim, Yussuf Alharoub, is not Jewish, but a Palestinian from Bethlehem. And one of his assailants was shot dead by security police. Yussuf told the *Ynet* news service: "Both the Jews and the Palestinians are suffering because of what's happening now and no-one benefits."

Jesus declared unequivocally that he is "the truth" (see John 14.6) and his beloved disciple John said that whoever hates his brother is in darkness (see 1 John 2.10), adding that those who denied that Jesus was the Messiah were liars (see 1 John 2.22). Jesus further claimed to be the gate to salvation, the Good Shepherd, and that all who came before him were thieves and robbers. "The thief comes only to steal and kill and destroy (sound familiar?); I have come that they may have life, and have it to the full" (John 10.10).

What we are witnessing across our warring world – from the new atheists and secular humanists in England to the Islamic fanatics in the Middle East – is a common thread of hatred for the God of Israel, whom Christians worship. The shocking truth is that in England, as in Saudi Arabia and Islamic State-controlled territory, there is no protection for Muslims who have found Jesus to be the true Shepherd.

Nissar Hussain, a British man of Pakistani descent, was brutally beaten outside his home in Bradford, Yorkshire. This followed nearly 20 years of harassment, intimidation, insults and physical abuse, along with attacks on his property and family members at the hands of the Muslim community, and in all of this he has been betrayed time and again by those who are there to protect him. Police, church leaders and political authorities have rigidly refused to concede that it is his status as a convert from Islam that has made him a target. Apparently none of them wanted to compromise their relationship with Muslims.

Now a British court has committed a travesty of justice in the case of appalling anti-Semitic abuse against a Jewish man at London's famous Speakers' Corner – a long-time icon to freedom of speech. Despite clear evidence of a whole gamut of racial abuse (which is illegal in Britain as a 'hate' crime), the perpetrator was found guilty only for damage to the victim's mobile phone which was knocked to the ground in the scuffle created by the incident. Yet in Northern Ireland (also part of the UK), Pastor Jim McConnell was put on trial for saying that Islam is 'Satanic'. (Fortunately, the eventual outcome was in his favour). As I have pointed out, it is a battle between light and darkness. Whose side are you on?

Dancing with the devil

While we are on the subject of Satanic darkness, I had been wondering whether we Westerners were reaping the consequences of 'dancing with the devil' even before I learnt that the main target of the Paris massacre was a theatre until recently owned by Jews.[2] That so many civilians enjoying an evening out should suddenly find themselves face to face with a virtual firing squad almost defies the imagination. It was an appalling attack on unsuspecting individuals which had all the hallmarks of Satan. But there was evidently an elephant in the room, a great unmentionable that dare not speak its name.

Boris Johnson, London Mayor at the time, referred to the perpetrators – Islamic State terrorists – as a 'death cult', which it certainly is. But what commentators seem deliberately to have missed – along with the Bataclan concert hall's Jewish connection – was the link between such evil extremism and the dark nature of the concert that claimed most of the lives lost. The *Eagles of Death Metal* band had apparently just started a song called *Kiss the devil*[3] when the gunmen opened fire and the auditorium morphed into the devil's domain. Fantasy became reality, with one witness describing it as "hell". I am not suggesting in any way that the victims had brought this disaster on themselves, but I am saying that Western society as a whole *is* partly responsible. For we have collectively lowered our guard against the demonic forces now unleashed with such ferocity by betraying our Judeo-Christian foundations.

The massacre in Manchester, mentioned earlier, also took place at a pop concert, with American star Ariana Grande singing: *"Tonight I'm making deals with the devil... And I know it's gonna get me in trouble...."* As her website and song lyrics make abundantly clear, Grande propagates what has been termed 'raunch culture', designed to liberate young girls from all sexual inhibitions. All this is highly offensive to Muslims – and so should it be for Christians! Though Christians do not react with acts of violence, we should be making it clear to Muslims that we deplore the sexualisation of our children.[4]

As for Paris, there was mention of prophecy in the *Mail on Sunday*, who recalled their earlier "prophetic" report headlined "Med boats' secret cargo: jihadis bound for Britain". The same paper also reported the "chilling prophecy" of a controversial film about a terrorist rampage in Paris – about to open in French cinemas – that was subsequently withdrawn in the wake of the actual thing happening instead. (It was also due to be screened earlier in 2015, but was pulled following the attacks on the *Charlie Hebdo* satirical magazine and Jewish supermarket.)

Hardly anyone in the media talks of biblical prophecy, however. Yet that would shed an awful lot of light on this dark subject! Just one example of this is that the world would be full of violence – as in the days of Noah – in the time immediately preceding the return of Jesus to set up his kingdom of peace. Politicians have referred to the Paris massacre as an 'attack on civilisation'. But my response is: what civilisation? We seem obsessed with dark and lurid fantasy, and with images of violence in our living rooms. We congratulate ourselves on our culture of 'freedom', bought at a great price in two world wars and, before that, with the blood of Christian martyrs who went to the stake for the cause of publishing God's Word, now discarded and thrown to the winds, only to be replaced by moral relativism where there are virtually no rules for living; where we promote death (through abortion and euthanasia, for example) and set about 'redefining' marriage, family and society as a whole.

Homophobia and Islamophobia are among the many politically-correct *don'ts* to have replaced the Ten Commandments. I have already mentioned the case of Jim McConnell, the highly-respected Northern Ireland preacher who stood trial on allegations of breaking the latter rule. It is possibly only a matter of time before we are denied the freedom of saying that Jesus is the only way to God (a claim he made about himself) for fear of offending other religions. But our civilisation was built on this very statement! We believed him, because he was totally authentic, and rose from the dead. We do not have to force anyone else to believe him; we simply declare the truth about him. Tragically, however, our moral defences are down, our walls have been breached, and the foundations of our Judeo-Christian civilization have been undermined. That is why we are wobbling as a society in grave danger of collapse.

I cannot speak for France and the rest of Europe, but as far as Britain is concerned, time is running out. The iconic Big Ben clock, which has become a symbol of the UK throughout the globe, has recently undergone repairs amidst fears that it is rapidly becoming beyond repair. It is, of course, part of the complex comprising our famous Houses of Parliament, which is itself in danger from crumbling foundations with talk of MPs possibly having to move out. Even some of our great houses, so loved by tourists, are under threat for lack of finance.

We were once a great nation sending missionaries around the world to share the life-changing (indeed, nation-changing) good news about Jesus. But now we have thrown out what was once most precious to us. Jesus told us to build on the rock. But we have built on sand.

Instead of building on the rock that has stood the test of time, the sure and certain foundation that is Christ, the certainty of his resurrection from the dead and his coming again to set up an everlasting kingdom, we have built on the shifting sand of appeasement, uncertainty and short-term comfort. But there is still hope. Our loving Saviour holds out arms of love, willing us to return from our self-imposed exile and, with Him, repair the walls that have broken down. Oh, that one of our leaders would call a national day of prayer! That is my prayer.

'Russian alliance places Israel in peril'

The peril in which Israel has been placed by Russia's new Middle Eastern alliances was highlighted at a London conference held in the shadow of the UK Parliament. Five years after the outbreak of the so-called Arab Spring, it was noted that Russia's new link with Iran, Iraq and Syria – sworn enemies of the Jewish state – was hardly a recipe for stability even if the intention was to deal effectively with the Islamic State terrorists.

Various leaders were addressing a gathering of Christian intercessors, linked with a campaign known as *Together for the Nation*, called to meet for urgent prayer (in light of grave crises facing the UK and the world) at the Emmanuel Centre in Westminster. Dr Clifford Hill, an eminent sociologist and author, repeated a statement made some years ago by a friend of his, the late Lance Lambert, that when the Shi'ite and Sunni streams of Islam have settled their differences, they would turn their attention to Israel. And British evangelist David Hathaway pointed out that in giving military backing to Syria and their allies, Vladimir Putin was supporting the bitter enemies of Israel – "currying favour with the very people who will launch the attack on Jerusalem," referring to a biblical prophecy of an Armageddon-style battle in the region (Ezekiel 38). He warned against Britain backing the wrong side – i.e. Putin – adding that getting rid of Saddam Hussein and Colonel Gadaffi had been big mistakes that had "unleashed the tiger" of Islamic fundamentalism.

Dr Hill also tackled the migrant crisis currently affecting Europe, which he believed could be the greatest opportunity ever for reaching Muslims with the gospel. He cited the case of Indonesia – the world's largest Islamic country – where millions had turned to Christ as a result of a government-sponsored migration programme in which people had been moved out of crowded cities onto islands populated by Christians. The warm welcome they received sparked a new-found faith, which has since spread like wildfire. In a similar way, he suggested, God could even bring good out of the evil of ISIS as ordinary Muslims are appalled by "behaviour which is on the model of Mohammed himself, who forced conversions and slaughtered Jews and Christians. But is the church ready for a great harvest?" he asked. A Congregational minister, Dr Hill is seriously concerned about growing secularisation in Britain, reflected in a catalogue of laws 'freeing' us from the constraints of biblical morality. Later in the day, he made a public confession for having neither said nor done anything at the time the 1967 Abortion Act was passed. "I was leading a congregation of one thousand in Tottenham, north London. I was too busy running church to see the bigger picture of what was happening in our nation."

Dangerous scenario must be seen through biblical lens

And so the stage is being set for what could turn into an almighty battle in the Middle East. Israel was already surrounded by sworn enemies before Russia entered the toxic fray, and we are now witnessing an extremely dangerous situation – highlighted by the blowing up of a plane over Sinai – which could erupt into a major conflict at any moment. But the entire scenario needs to be seen through a biblical lens. With such a focus, we should be in no doubt that this is a battle for truth more than anything else; it is not just a physical reality, but a spiritual certainty. The God of Israel is pitched against the old enemy, Satan, who is employing all his usual tricks in a bid to deceive the world with a torrent of lies.

Through the natural lens it may well appear as yet another young David facing up to the seemingly impossible task of slaying the nine-foot Philistine giant Goliath. But in fact David, through whose line Jesus traces his ancestry, never saw it that way: "You come against me with sword and spear and javelin, but I come against you in the name of the Lord Almighty, the God of the armies of Israel, whom you have defied" (1 Samuel 17.45). David became the greatest king Israel ever had, and today's reborn nation would do well to adopt their hero's total faith and trust in God.

True, today's Israeli society is as secular as Britain's in many ways. But there are encouraging signs that this could soon change. The prophets foretold that, before Messiah's return, there would be a great spiritual awakening among God's people whose hearts would be melted as they recognised the One who declared his everlasting love for them with outstretched arms.

The stage is set for this great unveiling, and the key is in the Word of God. Israel has miraculously survived many attempts to destroy her, but when the beleaguered nation finally takes her eyes off the 'horses and chariots' that have helped defend her thus far, they will surely put their total trust in the Lord. It is heartening to know that Prime Minister Netanyahu is a convinced believer in the Bible, which is well able to impart ultimate truth (2 Timothy 3.16) as he seeks the Lord on major decisions. We also hear of a colonel working to bring strong biblical values to IDF soldiers. A recent survey has revealed that an impressive 95% of Israelis have a Bible in their homes, and the heart of its message is: "Your word is a lamp to my feet and a light for my path" (Psalm 119:105). The Jewish people will very soon welcome their Messiah.

But the onus is not only on them. The Gentiles have a big responsibility to help in this process through their love and support, and indeed through sharing the message originally passed on to them by Jews like the Apostle Paul. In this respect Russia's establishing of a military base in the Syrian city of Latakia is a wake-up call to the Church. The city was known in ancient times as Laodicea, home of the first century church which earned a stern rebuke from our Lord that they were neither hot nor cold but lukewarm, and he was going to spit them out of his mouth. It is a good description of the Church's attitude to Israel's predicament today; they are neither hot nor cold about it; they simply cannot see its relevance to them. (See Revelation 3.14-22.)

Russia's presence, complete with tanks, ships and aeroplanes, was meant to prop up the Assad regime, a key ally of Iran which has made no secret either of its intention to wipe Israel off the map or of its support for the Hezbollah terrorists posing a major threat on Israel's northern borders. In fact, Iranian forces are now reported to be on the Golan Heights. The clash of interests is as obvious as it is frightening. All the while, tensions in Israel itself are almost at boiling point as I write, with seven children orphaned in recent attacks on innocent Jews.

Against this background the world continues to witness the deceit and hypocrisy of Palestinian leader Mahmoud Abbas who, at the UN, compared Israel to apartheid South Africa and Nazi Germany, and declared that the PA no longer considered itself bound by the 1993 Oslo Accords. Does this mean they are now officially terrorists again, as the Oslo Accords had legitimised them? The PA has never kept the agreement anyway, as their former leader Yasser Arafat was awarded the Nobel Peace Prize on the basis of dropping Israel's destruction from its charter. That never happened!

The raising of the PLO flag at the UN headquarters for the first time was about as effective as Goliath's shield. All that is needed is one well-aimed rock of God's truth and the whole sorry propaganda edifice will come crashing down as we all finally realise there never was a Palestinian people and that it was the Jews who were known as Palestinians before 1948. As bestselling author Jack Engelhard wrote at the time, "The entire world is arming itself against radical Islam, and it was to support radical Islam that Mahmoud Abbas came to the United Nations."[5]

The word of God says: "The day of the Lord is near for all nations. As you have done, it will be done to you; your deeds will return upon your own head" (Obadiah 1:15). Now Jew-hatred is effectively being exported to Europe, where many of the refugees fleeing Muslim countries will have been brought up on decades of anti-Semitism learned and promoted through schools, newspapers and social networks. Worse still, some of the refugees will undoubtedly turn out to be ISIS fighters in disguise.

Also in the Middle Eastern firing line are Christians, who worship Jesus, the Jew. I have just received a shocking report (from ASSIST News Service) of the beheading and crucifixion of a dozen indigenous Christian workers near Aleppo in Syria. Supported by US-based Christian Aid Mission, they had opportunities to escape, but chose to stay in order to provide aid and comfort in the name of Christ amidst the carnage. All were ex-Muslims who refused to renounce Christ, and were badly brutalised before being executed, with the two women among them publicly raped. Yet they prayed throughout their ordeal. In the midst of such unspeakable horror, the region's underground church has mushroomed since June 2014. One former ISIS fighter fled to Jordan where he intended to kill Christian aid workers. But something stopped him from following through with his plan, and that night he saw Jesus in a dream. He subsequently received Christ with tears, and now he is helping in the church. A spokesman said: "In the past we used to pray to have one person from a Muslim background come to the Lord. Now there are so many we can barely handle all the work among them."

Jews and Christians are in it together because they share their Messiah who is clearly coming soon, judging by the many signs of his imminent return. The nations are being shaken. It is time to stand with the God of Israel and the Israel of God!

Notes

[1] *kehilanews.com/category/community-blogs/israel-and-the-middle-east/*

[2] According to JNN News, quoting Arutz-7 radio, a member of the radical group Army of Islam told French security services back in 2011 that "we had planned an attack against the Bataclan because its owners are Jewish". It seems the perpetrators may not have known that the venue had recently changed hands. I have consistently stated in various articles that the ultimate target of Islamic State is the Jewish nation, referred to in a new video as the Muslims' No 1 enemy.

[3] Lyrics include: "Who'll love the devil? Who'll sing his song? I will love the devil and his song."

[4] See www.prophecytoday.uk article titled Wake-Up! written by Clifford Hill on June 2 2017.

[5] http://www.israelnationalnews.com/Articles/Article.aspx/17630#.VhY1w25VSuI

Chapter 23

Stealing God's Best Treasures

A scene from the movie *Woman in Gold* offers a graphic illustration of the plight faced by Israel today. As flowers are thrown at the invading Nazi soldiers in pre-war Vienna, no-one lifts a finger to help the real victims of the day – the Jewish people desperately trying to escape the brutality being meted out to them. The film, starring Helen Mirren, is based on a true story which powerfully reflects the extent to which anti-Semitism spreads its poisonous tentacles. Maria Altmann, who fled Austria for the United States when it was clear that Jewish citizens were in grave danger, discovered six decades later that her family had not only suffered the indignities of Nazi persecution, but had also been victims of the theft of art treasures, in particular a famous painting of her aunt – Adele Bloch-Bauer – which had effectively become Austria's 'Mona Lisa'.

Today Israel, and Jewish people the world over, are at least as vulnerable as they were under the Nazis; probably more so. Although now having a home of their own at last where they had hoped to live in peace and safety, they are constantly threatened on all sides by enemies looking to wipe them off the face of the earth! With the help of America – supposedly Israel's closest ally – Iran has effectively been freed to continue developing a nuclear weapon with which to carry out its stated aim of destroying Israel, while at the same time arming terrorist groups Hezbollah and Hamas, committed to the same goal. Tragically, history appears to be repeating itself. Former U.S. Vice-President Dick

Cheney and his daughter Liz have compared the nuclear deal between Iran and the six world powers to the Munich agreement which paved the way to World War II.[1] The Obama agreement – providing a pathway for the world's worst state-sponsor of terror to acquire nuclear weapons – is tragically reminiscent of British Prime Minister Neville Chamberlain's Munich treaty in 1938, they said. Each was negotiated from a position of weakness by a leader willing to concede nearly everything to appease an ideological dictator.

Dr Mike Evans, a close associate of Israeli leaders and founder of the Friends of Zion Heritage Centre in Jerusalem, writes: "Though the Obama Administration originally insisted on 'anytime, anywhere' inspections, they agreed to a deal that left Iran's military facilities off limits to any inspections and required 24 days' notice before inspections at other sites. Then we learned that no Americans could be part of any inspection team. Now comes word from Iran that the Iranian government will only allow International Atomic Energy Agency inspectors that they approve. If it were not so tragic, it would be humorous… but it is deadly serious, and the Jewish state and the Jewish people are at risk as never before."

A Jewish follower of Jesus who also reaches out a helping hand to destitute Holocaust survivors, Dr Evans adds: "On October 6, 1943, a delegation of American rabbis arrived at the White House for a personal audience with President Franklin Roosevelt. They planned to present irrefutable proof that the Nazis were conducting a wholesale annihilation of European Jews." But they were denied a meeting, no coordinated Allied rescue was launched, and the flames consumed six million Jews. Under Obama, America appeared to be ignoring appeals from Israel over Iran's plans to wipe out the Jews with atomic bombs, but thankfully Donald Trump has committed himself to taking appropriate action on this front. The Jewish people need to know that they are not alone; that their Christian friends around the world are standing with them.

"Iran's threats should be taken seriously," says James Woolsey, director of the Central Intelligence Agency during the Clinton Administration. "The people who have the mindset that they're just rhetoric are the same types of people who in the late 1920s and early 1930s said that Hitler's *Mein Kampf* was just rhetoric."[2]

But who, today, will lift a finger if Israel is invaded by her present enemies? Yet if she should return fire in defence, the wrath of the world may well fall on her. What utter hypocrisy! In short, what we are witnessing is age-old anti-Semitism, so often disguised as something noble, as with Western support for Palestinians portrayed as victims of bullying occupiers of their land – a land that rightfully belongs to Israel. Not only do they have a history there going back thousands of years, but it is God's gift to them (Genesis 12.7). If that is not good enough for our politicians, it is also theirs by international treaty signed in San Remo, Italy, in 1920. But Palestinians and their supporters are in the business of pulling the wool over our eyes and attempting to re-write history.

Another movie to which I keep returning is the 1958 classic musical *South Pacific*. With a score written by legendary Jewish combo Richard Rodgers and Oscar Hammerstein, it was not surprising that the race issue – raising its head in quite an ugly manner in America at the time – played a significant role in the context of romantic liaisons with Polynesian women. The script put it well, that people are "taught to hate" rather than born that way.

In the case of the so-called *Woman in Gold* painting, the Nazis had even stolen Adele Bloch-Bauer's identity in view of not wishing to disclose her real name because she was

Jewish. But with the help of a family member and struggling lawyer, her loyal niece successfully took the Austrian government to court. The painting was eventually taken to America and sold to a gallery there for $100 million, thereby achieving a degree of justice and restitution. But it was of little value compared with the heartache of parting from parents, and all she knew and loved, as Maria and her new husband were about to make their daring escape to freedom.

Followers of Jesus, the Jew, must not make the same mistake again, by effectively walking on the other side of the road as God's Chosen People are beaten up to within an inch of their collective lives. Now is the time to stand up and be counted, as Dr Evans is doing with his compassionate outreach to Holocaust survivors and others still scarred by the effects of the recent past.

Helen Mirren, by the way, is a dedicated supporter of Israel and recently hosted a prize-giving ceremony in the Land. "My connection to Israel and the Jewish people has truly been a part of making me what I am today, and I am very excited to be returning to this great country," she said. Though not Jewish, she has visited Israel many times and volunteered on a kibbutz in 1967. She has also campaigned against the Boycott, Divestment and Sanctions movement. Also, among her many film roles, she played an ex-Israeli Mossad agent in *The Debt*.

Notes

[1] *Wall Street Journal,* Friday 28 August 2015.

[2] The book outlining Hitler's political ideology.

ISRAEL'S GREAT FUTURE

Chapter 24

When Jesus Reveals Himself to His Brothers

I was greatly encouraged to read a report from David Lazarus in *Israel Today* about a group of prominent rabbis calling for a renewed look at Jesus. At the same time, I have been greatly inspired by a book about Joseph, the Jewish patriarch, and how he offered total forgiveness to his brothers who had sold him into slavery. *God Meant it for Good*[1] by R T Kendall was published by Kingsway 30 years ago, and is an absolute classic that could transform lives, communities and nations. The author's main purpose was to deal with the issue of forgiveness, so vital in all our dealings. But I want to deal with the issue of Joseph, as a type of the future Messiah, revealing himself to his brothers in the flesh, and of course forgiving them.

Effectively given up for dead, Joseph is finally unveiled – alive and in charge of all Egypt – and instead of wreaking vengeance by handing out the punishment they fully deserved, he astonishes them by saying: "You meant it for evil, but God meant it for good." (Genesis 50.20)

This is the gospel, and especially so for the Jew, to whom it was first given; that though we put Jesus on the cross – and the Jewish religious leaders were especially culpable – it was meant to happen. "...It was the Lord's will to crush him and cause him to suffer..." (Isaiah 53.10).

Despite his brothers' rejection, Joseph became the saviour of Israel, and was a sign of what would happen 400 years later when God's method of substitutionary sacrifice for sin was demonstrated on the night before the Exodus from

Egypt. Although Moses was the chosen human instrument in Israel's deliverance from slavery, the vital spiritual element was the blood of the lamb daubed on the lintels and doorposts of their homes, prefiguring the death of the Lamb of God who was to lead them into true freedom.

Joseph's brothers threw him down a well in a fit of jealousy over their father Jacob's misplaced favouritism. Thanks to Reuben's influence, they thought better of it and rescued him, only to sell him as a slave to passing Ishmaelites. But when, many years later, they were forced to go down to Egypt during the famine predicted by Joseph in interpreting Pharaoh's dream (of seven years of plenty followed by seven years of famine), they felt they were being punished for their wicked deeds and began to repent among themselves.

They did not at first recognise their brother, whose wisdom in hearing from God and thus storing up grain in preparation for the lean years was to save them from starvation, but of course it was a great shock when he was finally revealed as the Prime Minister of the greatest nation on earth! I imagine it was an even greater shock when they realised that he held nothing against them; that he wept with joy at being re-united with his brothers; and that they were totally forgiven.

It is interesting that Joseph was taken into Egypt after being rejected by his brothers. After Jesus was largely rejected by the Jewish people (though a significant number accepted him, of course, or the Church would never have come into existence), the message about him was taken to the nations, and the Gentile world elevated him to a prominent role in their affairs. Isaiah had prophesied that the Gentiles would put their hope in Him. (See Isaiah 42.4; see also Matthew 12.21.)

As far as the UK and the USA are concerned, it would be true to say that from the 17th to 19th centuries the gospel of

Christ and the Bible itself was the most influential teaching they possessed, affecting virtually every institution and producing great wealth and power in the process. At the same time, a host of passionate preachers went out to the far corners of the world, spreading this gospel to heathen nations. Jesus had in some respects become Lord of the Gentile world, a situation that would, in time, make Israel "envious", according to the Apostle Paul, an orthodox Jewish rabbi who led the mission to the Gentiles (see Romans 11.11).

But just as Joseph never forgot his brothers, and longed for reunion with them, so Jesus – actually descended from Judah and described in the Bible as the Lion of the tribe of Judah (see Rev 5.5), reaches out in love to his long-lost brothers in the flesh, for whom things got worse before they got better. Now, over the past two centuries (even in the midst of multiple pogroms and the Holocaust itself), He has been revealing himself afresh to his people.

Though, sadly, Jesus is still seen largely as God of the Gentiles, Jewish eyes have gradually been opened. It is believed, for example, that there were as many as 100,000 Jewish followers of Jesus at the outbreak of World War II in 1939.[2] Tragically, many of them would have perished in Hitler's gas chambers. But out of the ashes of the Holocaust, we not only have a reborn nation of Israel but a growing number of so-called Messianic fellowships who know and worship Jesus.

Just as Joseph was a sign of what was to come 400 years later with deliverance from Egypt through the blood of the lamb, so the voice of the prophets recorded in the Jewish Tenach (what Christians call the Old Testament) fell silent for 400 years until the revelation of Jesus in the New Testament. Joseph provided his brothers with grain amidst the famine. Now Jesus is "the bread of life" – the manna from heaven

– as he "fills the hungry with good things" (see John 6.35, Luke 1.53).

There will come a time when, back in the land of promise and delivered from bondage in a hostile world, all Israel will recognise Yeshua, their Messiah. (See Zechariah 12.10, Romans 11.26.) What a day that will be – life from the dead as he who was despised and rejected of men is revealed to his brothers alive… and as Lord of all!

Fig tree's fruit ready for harvest

At the time of the Jewish New Year, with the sweet taste of honey-dipped apple in many mouths, I was praying for Israel to have a fresh revelation of their destiny, and I was reminded of the fact that the Lord describes them as the apple of his eye (see Zechariah 2.8) for which he longs with an everlasting love. With the eye being the most sensitive part of the body, anticipating trouble almost before it happens, we can be sure that God is watching over his beloved at this particularly dangerous time.

I have written much about the signs of the Second Coming, but I was not expecting to get one during a visit to family in leafy Hampstead, north London. Walking up a pathway I have used for the past 47 years, I suddenly noticed the spreading branches of an overhanging fig tree. It was like the one we had in our garden in South Africa, but I had never seen one in this part of the world before. What particularly struck me was that it was laden with fruit, almost ripe for harvest.

I was reminded of the words of Jesus in describing the signs of his imminent return. "Now learn this lesson from the fig-tree: As soon as its twigs get tender and its leaves come out, you know that summer is near. Even so, when you see these things happening, you know that it is near, right at the door. I tell you the truth, this generation will certainly not pass away until all these things have happened" (Mark 13.28-30).

The fig tree is used in the Bible as a symbol for Israel. So it seems the Lord was saying that when it started to blossom – i.e. Israel's long-promised restoration to their land and their subsequent growth into a vibrant nation state – we would know that his coming was not far away. Yet this Hampstead tree was not simply in blossom; it was almost ready for harvest. It was, after all, late summer. Was God perhaps speaking to my heart, saying that Israel's salvation – that is, her full restoration, both physically and spiritually – was about to happen; that we are about to witness a bountiful harvest among his chosen people in the form of a mass recognition of Yeshua as their long-awaited Messiah who, with loving arms, is coming to rescue them from their many enemies? Are we about to witness the spiritual restoration, following their return to the land, spoken of by Ezekiel: "I will give you a new heart and put a new spirit in you; I will remove from you your heart of stone and give you a heart of flesh" (Ezek 36.26)?

In the passage quoted earlier, Jesus suggests that the generation witnessing the physical restoration of Israel, along with signs from heaven and increasing turbulence on earth, would also see its spiritual rebirth and the return of Christ himself. Adding further intrigue to this scenario was the completion in autumn 2015 of a very rare *tetrad* – four successive blood-red moons visible during Israel's key festivals of Passover and Sukkot (Tabernacles), with a total eclipse of the sun having occurred halfway through this phenomenon. Remember, Jesus said that immediately preceding his coming, "the sun will be darkened and the moon will not give its light" (Mark 13.24). My friends, no-one knows the day or hour, but of this we can be sure: Jesus is coming again – and very soon it seems!

Israel's significance in all this cannot be overstated and was re-emphasised to me the day after my Hampstead stroll as I was admiring the Savill Garden on the Queen's estate near Windsor. I took a series of pictures of the beautiful borders and, when I viewed them later, was mystified by one of the 'photos' which seemed to have a Star of David – Israel's national emblem – imprinted against a murky grey background. Make of that what you will. Then, in the early hours one morning, I heard a still, small voice asking me to be a 'doorkeeper' in the house of the Lord. I took that as confirmation of a calling to continue watching for signs of his coming, and convey that to readers.

As Haggai predicted, everything is being shaken in preparation for the return of Messiah (see Haggai 2.6f). Tens of thousands of refugees, possibly including jihadist infiltrators, are swarming into Europe, putting huge pressure on EU countries already creaking under the weight of increasing political, social and economic upheavals. Yet no-one asks why Saudi Arabia, which has both the economic and physical capacity to take them, has so far completely failed to do so. The Gulf state is reported to have 100,000 air-conditioned tents, capable of housing three million people, sitting empty – used only for five days each year to accommodate pilgrims to Mecca.

Meanwhile, Britain has been severely jolted by the election of an extreme-leftist as leader of Her Majesty's Opposition. At his first public engagement, Jeremy Corbyn even refused to sing 'God save the Queen', the national anthem. The UK's 290,000 Jews – already under increasing attack from anti-Semites – now fear a Labour leader who has referred to Hamas and Hezbollah as 'friends'. What on earth is going on?

But be comforted, O Israel, for all this trouble also points to hope, when the glory of the Lord will be revealed (see

Isaiah 40.5) and Yeshua HaMashiach (Jesus, the Messiah) will return.

"I have chosen you and have not rejected you. So do not fear, for I am with you; do not be dismayed, for I am your God. I will strengthen you and help you; I will uphold you with my righteous right hand… those who oppose you will be as nothing and perish" (Isaiah 41.9-11).

Killing of innocents could be significant

The massacre of innocent children that we have been witnessing in recent days, although a ghastly reflection of the merciless brutality of which humans are capable, could also be a prelude to a highly significant global phenomenon. In biblical terms such atrocities preceded some of the greatest events in world history and is symbolically depicted as the great dragon (Satan) attempting to wreak destruction before the new order has had a chance to breathe. For example, in Revelation 12.4 we read: "The dragon stood in front of the woman who was about to give birth, so that he might devour her child the moment it was born." I believe this speaks particularly about the exile from slavery in Egypt of the ancient Israelites, the coming of the Jewish Saviour at the time of King Herod, the rebirth of modern Israel, and now the spiritual re-awakening of the Chosen People.

Each of the first three was preceded by the killing of innocents – the baby Moses was hidden in the bulrushes of the Nile to escape the sword of a Pharaoh alarmed by the rapid growth of the Jewish population; Jesus escaped with his parents to Egypt before Herod ordered the slaughter of all boys under the age of two in the vicinity of Bethlehem on learning of the new-born King of the Jews; and the Nazis sent six million Jews, including one-and-a-half million children, to their deaths in the concentration camps, just as a Jewish homeland was on the brink of becoming reality.

More recently we heard of the mowing down by the Taliban of 130 schoolchildren in Peshawar, Pakistan, at the same time Christian children in Iraq were being butchered in front of their parents by ISIS terrorists for refusing to deny Jesus. In fact, everywhere children are the victims of shocking brutality, with millions slaughtered in the womb in an increasingly godless world where life has become cheap and a culture of death prevails.

The dragon tries to snatch the baby at birth, knowing the effect he would have on the world, but ultimately fails. In the same way in more recent times he tried to prevent the rebirth of Israel, an essential prerequisite for the return to earth of Jesus, according to the Bible. When the Nazis' attempted extermination of European Jews stopped short of its target, the Arab nations surrounding the new Jewish state declared war on Israel on the very day it was born in 1948. Every subsequent attempt to wipe Israel off the map (the avowed intention of all Islamic fundamentalists) has ultimately failed – witness 1967, 1973 and the constant provocation from terrorists backed by many of the world's politicians.

But now we stand on the brink of the last great sign to herald the soon return of Christ – the spiritual rebirth of Israel when Jewish people en-masse recognise "the one they have pierced" (see Zechariah 12.10) as their Messiah in fulfilment of the ancient Scriptures. More and more Jews are discovering the reality of who Jesus is, while others among them are becoming increasingly open to the possibility of him being their Messiah.

The devil knows his time is short, so he is applying unprecedented pressure on Israel in order to intimidate its people and break their spirit. The murder of children is shocking and tragic, but I believe we could soon be witnessing a great harvest of Jews (and Arabs) deciding to follow Yeshua who will also soon make his long-awaited re-appearance in Jerusalem when every knee will bow, and every tongue confess, that Jesus is Lord.

Notes

[1] Newly titled *Total Forgiveness* in reprinted editions.

[2] *Restoring Israel* by Kelvin Crombie, published by Nicolayson's Ltd, Christ Church, Jerusalem, page 156.

Chapter 25

The Reason for Romans

The Apostle Paul, in his long letter to the Roman Christians, declared: "I am not ashamed of the gospel, because it is the power of God for the salvation of everyone who believes: first for the Jew, then for the Gentile" (Romans 1.16f).

Wherever he went on his great missionary journeys, his first port of call was always the synagogue, which actually followed the pattern set by his Master.

I believe the church in Britain seems as a whole to have lost its sharp focus on mission. Where is the emphasis on evangelism that was once such an integral part of British evangelicalism, when Billy Graham was so much part of the scene? One thing seems clear to me: that when we take our eyes off the primacy of the gospel, we also lose our focus on the place of the Jews in God's purposes. Along with the revivals of the 18th and 19th centuries came a renewed understanding of our relationship to the Jews. After all, Jesus told the woman at the well that "salvation is from the Jews" (John 4.22).

In the case of the Roman believers, Paul mentions that he had planned to visit them many times, but had so far been prevented. As we now know, he was eventually taken there as a prisoner, though he was free to preach there for two years.

At over 7,000 words, Paul's epistle to the Romans was probably the longest letter ever written in the ancient world. It would have been a very expensive undertaking and, given that Paul rarely interfered with work he had not started, its message must have been highly significant in that particular situation as well as to us (as with all Scripture). He is addressing two distinct groups within the church – Jews and Gentiles. Why is this?

It seems this church had been established by Jews who were present on the Day of Pentecost. But some 16-20 years later, in 49 AD, Rome's 40,000 Jews were expelled by Claudius. That is why Paul first met Priscilla and Aquila in Corinth – "because Claudius had ordered all Jews to leave Rome" (Acts 18.2). Naturally, the Gentiles then stepped into the shoes of the absent leaders. But just six years later, following the death of Claudius, Jews were invited back by the new emperor, Nero, who rightly reckoned they were good for business. Tensions had arisen by the time Paul was writing. Some of it was over whether certain days and feasts should continue to be celebrated, but there were also much greater issues at stake.

To the Jews among them, Paul emphasises that, though the law is good, it won't save them, and that it needed to be written on their hearts (Romans 2.15 and v. 28). He stresses that "all have sinned", but that we are justified by grace through faith. He discusses our constant struggle with sin. Again, the law is good – without it we would not have known what sin was – but Jesus rescues us from this predicament. "Therefore, there is now no condemnation for those who are in Christ Jesus…" (8.1). To the Gentiles among them, he explains that just because we are not under law but under grace, that does not mean we can continually get away with sin. "For the wages of sin is death…" (6.23).

But because I believe British Christians in particular need to hear this, I want to concentrate on what Paul reminded the Gentiles of: firstly, that though he was an apostle to the Gentiles who, according to Isaiah, would put their hope in the Jewish Messiah, God had not finished with the Jews (Isaiah 11.10). True, the 'Rock' of Christ was to prove a stumbling block (9.33). They were blinded in part so that

Jesus would be crucified; otherwise we would have had no Saviour to atone for our sins. There was a sense that the Jewish religious leaders, in collusion with Rome, had done us a favour by sending Jesus to the cross. Indeed, Paul would write: "And we know that in all things God works for the good of those who love him, who have been called according to his purpose" (Rom 8.28).

But let us not forget that a significant remnant – 500 who witnessed Jesus' resurrection, 3,000 more on the Day of Pentecost and an estimated 100,000 (half the population of Jerusalem) within a generation – did repent, believe in Jesus and had received the Spirit, and told the world, spreading the gospel through Paul and the other apostles, witnesses and evangelists.

It was never God's intention that the Church should cut itself off from its Hebraic root. For in doing so they were no longer sharing "in the nourishing sap from the olive root" (see 11.17) – pretty disastrous, effectively leaving the tree to wither and die. That is what happened to the Church and led to the 'Dark Ages' with little understanding of the Scriptures. Christianity progressively developed into Churchianity, and some sections of this 'church' became the chief persecutors of the Jewish people. Some even today who claim to be Christian have become haters of Israel, and tragically much of the Western Church has fallen for a deceptive line where, at best, they opt for a neutral stand on the issue of Israel. But in fact Paul urges us against arrogance, thundering: "You do not support the root, but the root supports you" (11.18).

Not only that, but God has a wonderful future plan for his people, spelled out in chapters 9-11 where Paul goes to great lengths to explain how it was only the mercy of God that allowed us to be partakers with them of the heavenly kingdom. "Because of their transgression, salvation has come to the Gentiles ... to make Israel envious. But if their transgression means riches for the world, and their loss means riches for the Gentiles, how much greater riches will their fullness bring! I am talking to you Gentiles" (11.11-13). When the full number of Gentiles has come in, all[1] Israel will be saved (11.25f). But that does not excuse us from the responsibility of preaching the gospel to them (10.12-14), for all – both Jew and Gentile – must come through Jesus (3.22f). Yes, there is much value to being a Jew, Paul argues, but it won't save you. Justification is on the principle of faith, "apart from observing the Law" (see 3.27f.). This even applied to Abraham, who was righteous before he was circumcised (4.10).

Nevertheless, Paul says, "You…have now received mercy as a result of their disobedience…" (11.30). Therefore (chapter 12 begins), in view of God's mercy…the blessings of Israel have been extended to you. By no means have you replaced them. The blessing has been extended – in view of God's mercy. "You do not support the root, but the root supports you." Because God has been so merciful, "offer your bodies as living sacrifices" and "do not conform any longer to the pattern of this world...." It is obvious from the context that Paul is particularly referring to the need for believers to abstain from sexual immorality (which was so rife in Rome, a hotbed of forbidden sexual practices where many of the emperors engaged in what today would be called bisexual activity, in defiance of God's one-flesh ordinance. Paul had already (in the opening chapter) taught about this matter at length. This is another of the book's great themes. Rome was a civilisation rapidly descending into an immoral abyss, like Britain today. In chapter 1 Paul referred to the 'shameful lusts' and how, because much of the populace had denied the existence of God, they had cast off all restraint (not believing they would ever be accountable for their sin) and became immersed in every kind of depravity and wickedness. If you think Paul was exaggerating, consider the fact that, shortly after writing this letter (in AD 79), Mt Vesuvius erupted and buried Pompeii in lava, suffering the same fate as Sodom and Gomorrah. Some of the believers had previously indulged in this, and the reason they were being so persecuted (with worse to come) was because they now refused to go with the flow of society's sinful behaviour. The response of the crowd was: 'How dare you condemn what we're doing as sinful?' Does that ring any bells? This is certainly the case in Britain today where preachers are being hauled before the courts for daring to criticise immoral acts that are dragging the nation down into a pit of degradation. We can expect the persecution to get worse. It inevitably will in such a mighty clash of cultures. This is why another great theme of Romans is suffering. Under Nero, Christians were thrown into a sports arena, covered in animal skins to be torn apart by dogs, or crucified and set on fire. Yet, in the face of all this, they were being encouraged to stand up and be counted: "If God is for us, who can be against us? (8.31) ... Who shall separate us from the love of Christ? Shall trouble or hardship or persecution or famine or nakedness or danger or sword? As it is written, 'For your sake we face death all day long; we are considered as sheep to be slaughtered.' No, in all these things we are more than conquerors through him who loved us. For I am convinced that neither death nor life, neither angels nor demons, neither the present nor the future, nor any powers, neither height nor depth, nor anything else in all creation, will be able to separate us from the love of God that is in Christ Jesus our Lord" (8.35-39).

So, in view of God's plan to redeem his people who, we are told, will accept their Messiah in great numbers before his return, we need to become part of that restoration – i.e. help it come about, by which I mean getting ourselves re-focused on the gospel, especially on reaching the Jews! In his lengthy passage expressing his earnest prayer for Israel to be saved, Paul asks: "How can they believe in the one of whom they have not heard?" (10.14) Paul was not to know how disastrously the Church would break away from its Hebraic root, leading to many centuries of spiritual darkness, which has made it even more difficult for Jews to believe a gospel they have long associated with being treated as lambs to the slaughter and being expelled from their adopted countries (as were my ancestors). As Helen Shapiro challenged folk in Yorkshire, they need to be persuaded against holding on to the understandable notion that we Christians have always been their persecutors. They need to know that the gospel is actually good news! Quite apart from anything else, we owe it to them. Towards the end of the letter, Paul says he is on his way to Jerusalem with a gift of money for the poor among the saints there. The gift came from the Gentile Christians of Macedonia and Achaia, of whom Paul says: "They were pleased to do it, and indeed they owe it to them; for if the Gentiles have shared in the Jews' spiritual blessings, they owe it to the Jews to share with them their material blessings" (see 15.27). There are still poor in Israel – many of them make an economic sacrifice to live there because the cost is living is high and income is relatively low. But they desperately need spiritual refreshing too, which only the gospel can provide. If you cannot preach to them, pray for them, love them, bless them, speak up for them and seek God for better understanding of their plight.

The gospel is for the Jew first. But with privilege comes responsibility. The Jew will also be first to be judged for wrongdoing (see 2.9-11). Nevertheless, God has not rejected his people; he has a great plan for them, and you can be part of that.

Note

[1] I am reliably informed that the Hebraic sense of the word translated *all* is *a vast number.*

Chapter 26

The Key to Divine Deliverance

Israel's plight of being hemmed in on all sides by mortal enemies seems a particularly pitiful one. But in one sense it is the best possible place for them to be, as the miracle of the first Passover reminds us. Having seen their firstborn survive a plague of death through the blood of a lamb daubed on the doorposts of their houses, the way was now open for the Jews to escape slavery in Egypt as Pharaoh finally had his fill of disasters.

Sure, the blood of the lamb was the key to their salvation, but they needed to keep trusting the God of Israel for every step of their path to the Promised Land. The first surprise was that a short cut was not the best route. That would have taken them through Philistine country, and God did not want them to face war so early because it would discourage them. Instead he led them to an area where they were completely trapped, hemmed in by the desert on one side and the sea on the other, with Pharaoh's troops (having changed their minds about losing services of the Hebrew people) now chasing down hard on their heels.

So it is with us. God takes us on a circuitous route in our discipleship for a reason. When we find ourselves trapped and hemmed in on all sides, we are in Position A for a miracle. The Israelites panicked, but Moses said: "Do not be afraid. Stand firm and you will see the deliverance the Lord will bring you today" (Exodus 14.13). He goes on: "The Egyptians you see today you will never see again. The Lord will fight for you; you need only to be still" (v14).

A little while ago, I was due to make an 80-mile round trip to interview a friend for another book I am working on. But I had to go via a certain town for a dental appointment, so that added to the distance. However, my main obstacle was a series of roadworks which meant several big diversions, so that in the end I clocked up 120 miles through every county in Yorkshire (north, south, east and west). We can all get impatient with road delays, but I am sure God is at work in those too, perhaps teaching us patience, for one thing. Perhaps he also wants to show us some magnificent new vistas showcasing his beautiful handiwork! As it happened, I went through some lovely villages we used to cover when I was the newspaper editor in that district 30 years ago, and yet I never visited them at the time as we relied on local residents to send us their news. The roadworks may be a short-term problem, but they are a long-term benefit. God may not want you to go down certain paths, perhaps because they are dangerous, or maybe he is smoothing out the highway for you so that, when the time is right, you will be able to drive through unhindered. I was over half-an-hour late for my friend, but he had dozed off while waiting in his car, so obviously benefitted from a needful and refreshing sleep. Nothing is wasted with God.

St Paul's journey of discipleship took him via prison, from where he wrote the most joyful of his epistles, calling on the Philippians to "rejoice in the Lord always". I have a friend who has been in prison these past three years (and in my opinion he is the victim of gross injustice), and his letters are very upbeat. Referring to the regular visits he receives, unlike most of his fellow inmates, he wrote: "I am so blessed!" In another letter he wrote: "All through the last two years I have been kept safe and well, with a strong realisation that God is in charge of what's happening, not man, nor me! It's just the path he's taking me on, though a very unusual one."

God wants us to trust him for every move we make. The fearful Israelites were about to witness one of the greatest miracles of history; indeed, a picture of the coming resurrection of their Messiah Yeshua – and of all who follow him. They were as good as dead; Pharaoh's forces actually overtook them as they camped by the sea near Pi Hahiroth, opposite Baal Zephon. No wonder they were terrified. But Moses said, "Don't panic!" And then he said, "Stand firm" (also translated "Stand still").

True enough, they were trapped; they had nowhere to go. That is just where God wanted them. He wanted them to go to him! There will never be a situation when a believer has nowhere to go; even if he is trapped in a war zone or a concentration camp, God is there. Notice that Moses' instruction is not to retreat or do anything, but to "stand still" and let God do the work. He will bring about the miracle, but not if we interfere by trying to manipulate the situation, for that would be trusting in our own 'good' deeds to win God's favour. In situations like this, don't touch anything or do anything; just raise your hands to God in prayer, and let him work the miracle. God will fight for you.

How desperately we believers need to learn this lesson about taking our hands off the 'ark' of God's presence. Remember when Uzzah tried to steady the Ark as it was being taken back to Jerusalem. He was struck down dead (see 1 Chronicles 13.9f). We like to help God along with our puny efforts, but he doesn't need them. He only wants our perfect trust. Abraham, despite his legendary faith, could not quite believe that God could provide a son through the aged Sarah, so he thought he would give the Lord a hand by having sex with Hagar, and look what happened! We are still suffering the consequences through the ongoing Arab-Jewish conflict.

I remember going through a very difficult time in my youth involving marriage, family and future, calling out to the Lord from the beautiful Yorkshire hills where I used to walk, and hearing the still, small voice of God saying: "Stand still, and see the salvation of your God!" In time the Lord brought me through into verdant green pastures, but his timing is also vital as, over and over again since then, I have experienced the miracle of God's perfect timing – not a moment too soon, and not a moment too late, as I usually discover afterwards. I have found that music so often plays a part. I don't know why that is; perhaps it is because I so love praising and worshipping God as I go about my business that sometimes the Lord speaks back to me in song.

There was a time when I was struggling over issues concerning production of an evangelistic tabloid I started called *New Life*. As I anxiously mulled over the problems while driving to our offices, words of the famous Andrew Lloyd-Webber song *Memory* – "I must think of a new life, and I mustn't give in…"[1] – came over the car's audio-cassette player and soothed my soul in a way I shall never forget.

On another occasion I was writing of my experiences in Israel for my book *Peace in Jerusalem* when I recalled the encouragement I felt as I passed a man singing the Leonard Cohen hit *Hallelujah* on the pavement of Zion Square. At that precise moment, classical singer Katherine Jenkins struck up on my CD player with the very same song! I had forgotten it was on that album.

A third example of this occurred more recently during another turbulent time. I was writing an article entitled *Bread of Heaven* for a website I had joined (Scriggler.com), and not really sure I was doing the right thing. But as I was in the process of actually writing the words 'bread of heaven', a symphony of male voices echoed those very words – 'Bread of heaven, bread of heaven, feed me now and evermore!' –

from the well-known hymn *Guide me, O thou great Jehovah* sung during a recording for a Robin Mark album.[2]

I was ecstatic. The timing could not have been more perfect, and that is just it. You know that it is God when you have not manipulated anything, and it is so very encouraging. So wait for it, as the Lord urged the prophet Habakkuk when he was seeking to know why the wicked prospered. The hymn just mentioned is particularly apt in our discussion about God guiding us to the Promised Land, and includes the line "I am weak, but thou art mighty, hold me with thy powerful hand...."

Yet even after he has taken us across the Red Sea as on dry land, and we have watched our pursuing enemies drown as the waters sweep over them, the journey to Canaan is not a quick one. Yes, they could have got there much sooner, but it took 40 years of wandering in the wilderness. And that was not a mistake either, for it was there that they learnt to trust in the God who provides manna from heaven and water from the Rock, and that "man does not live on bread alone, but on every word that proceeds from the mouth of the Lord" (Deuteronomy 8.3).

I have followed the Lord now for 46 years, and I can assure you that nothing, and no experience, is wasted if you are determined to be where God wants you. The frightened Israelites were hemmed in on all sides, but the sea opened up when they obeyed Moses' words to "stand still" and see the salvation of their God. The shackles of slavery were finally broken, and the joy of freedom was powerfully extolled in the songs of Moses and Miriam: "I will sing to the Lord, for he is highly exalted... Who is like you – majestic in holiness, awesome in glory, working wonders? In your unfailing love you will lead the people you have redeemed. In your strength you will guide them to your holy dwelling" (see Exodus 15.1, 11, 13). That same joy and freedom can be ours too.

The crossing of the Red Sea is a picture of the death and resurrection of Christ, and indeed a precursor of the baptism rite as believers identify with their Messiah's death and suffering by total immersion in water before being raised up (by the baptiser) to new life, a physical symbol of what has happened in the spiritual realm. Of course, only the God-ordained miracle of a wall of water making way for the Israelites to cross prevented their total immersion, and when they landed safely on the other side, it was as if they had been raised from the dead. St Paul writes of believers "... having been buried with him [Christ] in baptism and raised with him through your faith in the power of God, who raised him from the dead." (Colossians 2.12) He also talks of their Jewish forefathers "being baptized into Moses" in an obvious reference to the Red Sea crossing. (1 Corinthians 10.2)

Yet Israel *is* now in the Promised Land, where they should be safe and sound. But they are still hemmed in on all sides! The Jewish longing for what often seems the elusive hope of an eternal place of refuge has been beautifully expressed by some of their great modern composers and lyricists. But even in Israel the Jews are once again trapped, with nowhere to go, but to God. "Then fly to His side (to adapt the lyrics from South Pacific's *Some Enchanted Evening*) and make Him your own, or all through your life you will dream all alone!" The lamb slaughtered for the enslaved Jews is now fulfilled by the Lamb of God, slain for the sins of the world, who "for the joy set before him endured the cross, despising its shame, and is seated at the right hand of the throne of God" (Hebrews 12.2).

Joy in the midst of pain and suffering has become a hallmark of the Jew (and the Christian for that matter), who in the past has escaped from the chains of slavery to freedom of worship and victory over enemies. But there is a greater escape at hand. The pathway through the current sea of trouble has already been opened up by Yeshua HaMashiach, who has paid for our sins, according to the Scriptures, and was raised from the dead as the first-fruits of all who belong to him (see 1 Corinthians 15.20, 23). The miracle of the Passover works both ways – positively for those who put their trust in the blood of the Lamb, but disastrously for those who despise the One whom God the Father has sent to be our Saviour.

My wife and I recently enjoyed a wonderful meal at one of England's oldest coaching inns, the Lion Hotel in Buckden, Cambridgeshire. Built in 1492, it was once known (I am not sure why, but I can guess) as the *Lion and the Lamb*. That sounds like a description of Yeshua, the Lion of the tribe of Judah and the Lamb of God, as I explained to our waitress. He is the King of the Universe, not to be messed with, but also the innocent, suffering servant, slain for the sins of the world. If we repent before God, believe in Jesus (Yeshua) whose blood was shed for us on the cross, go on believing and trusting Him, and are baptized in water and the Holy Spirit, we will be saved for all eternity, entering into the joy of his kingdom. Yes, we are living in dark days, and worse still may lie ahead, but the best is yet to come.

Notes

[1] From the musical *Cats*.

[2] Robin Mark is a renowned worship leader and musician from Northern Ireland. The album is *The Mandate – Experiencing God* (Kingsway Music).

Chapter 27

The Power of Passover

For the past four years I have enjoyed the immense privilege of sharing, with hundreds of schoolchildren in my home town, the story of how Jesus, a Jewish rabbi, celebrated Passover with his disciples shortly before his trial after booking a large Upper Room in Jerusalem's Old City for the occasion. I had to re-tell the story dozens of times to a total of more than a thousand pupils aged six to eleven over seven days as part of engaging the kids with Christian teaching about Easter – that we see it as the fulfilment of Passover, which often happens to coincide with the Jewish festival.

They sat in rapt attention as I explained how, at this 'Last Supper', Jesus instituted what has become known to Christians as Holy Communion. But it was a Passover meal much like that celebrated by Jews today, except that when it came to the third of the traditional four cups of wine poured out (known as the 'cup of redemption'), he made the startling declaration: "This is my blood of the new covenant, which is poured out for many for the remission of sins. Do this, as often as you drink it, in remembrance of me."

We believe he was about to be sacrificed as the ultimate Passover Lamb, of which all previous feasts were only a foretaste. He added that he would not drink again of the fruit of the vine "until that day when I drink it anew in the kingdom of God" (Mark 14.24).

Yeshua also broke bread with his disciples, saying, "This is my body." The unleavened bread used by Jews today (matzos) is full of tiny holes, with darker stripes on the back, possibly indicating that the body of Yeshua was pierced by cruel nails holding him to the cross while his back was as a ploughed field beaten by whips. Isaiah surely prophesies about this day when he writes: "He was pierced for our transgressions, he was crushed for our iniquities; the punishment that brought us peace was upon him, and by his wounds we are healed" (Isaiah 53.5).

Possibly with the cross in mind, Moses was instructed to tell the Israelites that the Lord would redeem his people "with an outstretched arm" (Exodus 6.6). As he hung in agony of soul and body on that cross outside the walls of ancient Jerusalem, we are told that Yeshua accepted the offer of a final drink from a soldier who, significantly I would say, used the stalk of a hyssop plant to dip a sponge in a jar of wine vinegar with which to wet the lips of the victim. The Israelites had been instructed to use hyssop to daub the lamb's blood on their doorposts before being freed from 400 years of slavery in Egypt. Was Yeshua here partaking of the fourth cup – the cup of completion – before declaring "It is finished" and breathing his last?

His cousin, John the Baptist, had declared of him a few years earlier: "Behold, the Lamb of God, who takes away the sin of the world" (John 1.29). We believe that all those wishing to have their sins 'passed over' must avail themselves of Yeshua's blood, figuratively 'marking' it on their hearts as protection from eternal destruction and a guarantee of life everlasting.

I will leave the last word in this section to Reform Rabbi Evan Moffic of the Solel Congregation in Chicago who, in his book *What every Christian needs to know about Passover*, notes that: "the shank bone symbolizes the lamb offered as a sacrifice at the Temple in Jerusalem 2,000 years ago. The lamb symbolizes God's mercy in redeeming the Israelites from slavery in Egypt. In Christian tradition, the lamb symbolizes Jesus, the Lamb of God, whose sacrifice frees believers from the sins of the world."

Hear O Israel: God is speaking!

Having grown accustomed to new household duties since my retirement, I was rather aggrieved by the sight of dirty footprints all over the kitchen floor. It was only when my wife returned home after a day's teaching that I was able to confirm 'whodunnit'. I was at least glad some stray animal had not wandered in seeking winter warmth. Linda explained that, before leaving for work, she had taken several trips into our wet and muddy back garden to avail herself of some foliage with which to teach her class about the Feast of Tabernacles (Sukkot), celebrating God's protection, provision and presence during Israel's 40 years in the wilderness. For the past 22 years she has been employed by a number of churches in the town to help local primary schools fulfil their curriculum as far as learning about Christianity and Judaism is concerned.

The children especially like learning about the Jewish feasts because it always seems to involve food. Linda regularly teaches about Passover and Shabbat, and you would think the kids had not eaten at home by the way they tuck into her lovingly-baked challah (traditional Jewish bread). Typically, among young children, they were not quite so eager to accept an orange apiece (substituting an *etrog* citron fruit) on another occasion.

On the very day these 11-year-olds were contemplating the meaning of these symbols, I received an email from an Australian friend all about Sukkot. Actually, the autumn feast was months away, but my friend Martin was trying to interest people in a tour to Israel he was organising, timed to coincide with the completion of the rare *tetrad* of blood moons to which I have already referred. (My wife's focus on

Sukkot was dictated by the school's agenda). Anyway, blood moons are generally regarded with alarm by soothsayers and prophets, and there has been a lot of trouble in Israel over the past year or so. But there is hope too! It is certainly a wake-up call for Jewish people to rise up and return to the God of their fathers and the word of the prophets, to seek His ways and commands as never before. The initiative launched by the Israeli government aimed at getting all its citizens to read the Bible needs to be taken up with relish. Therein lies hope for the future.

The people I pity most are not the victims of persecution, but those who refuse to obey God's commands and who curse Israel as a result. They have no future. Take the Tesco chain in Britain, for example. Founded by Jewish businessman Jack Cohen, it rose to become a grocery giant until political correctness got the better of its managers. Charitable giving was switched from cancer research to the promotion of homosexuality, and at least one store did little to prevent BDS (Boycott, Divestment and Sanctions) campaigners from placing yellow stickers on Israeli products. This was followed by the closure of stores all over the country with the loss of hundreds of jobs.

We need to get back to the Bible and remember that "man does not live on bread alone but on every word that comes from the mouth of the Lord". Through the Bible, we can hear the voice of God for ourselves. Remember how He spoke personally to the young Samuel, calling him three times before his master realised it must be God. Samuel did not at first recognise that it was the Lord, for that comes by persevering prayer and meditation on the Word until it becomes like breathing. Through the Bible, we converse with our Lord until it becomes second nature and our worldview is shaped entirely by this conversation with the fount of all wisdom who knows the end from the beginning. But we must get away from the call of mobile phones and the social media frenzy that demands our constant attention. Switch off the things of this world, and switch on to God. The Lord will keep us on track if we listen out for his voice, judging all we see, hear and read in the light of Scripture.

Listening to God, and doing what he says, is probably the surest way, not only to maintain your peace in the midst of storms, but also to fulfil God's best plans for you, and all those you will undoubtedly influence. As the Word of God brought creation into being, so will it bring to birth a renewal of our relationship with Elohim.[1] After all, we are here today and gone tomorrow. Isaiah writes: "All men are like grass, and all their glory is like the flowers of the field; the grass withers and the flowers fall, but the word of the Lord stands forever" (Isaiah 40.6-8).

Note

[1] An alternative Hebrew name for God.

Chapter 28

End-time Role for Jews and Gentiles

So the restoration of Israel continues. It was in no way completed by the creation of the modern state in 1948. That was just Part One. The Jewish population (of Israel) has since increased tenfold to over six million, passing the number lost in the Holocaust. Much of this boom is the result of immigration as Jews around the world have felt a 'home-call', or are fleeing persecution. Some of it could never have been foreseen as, for instance, a flood of immigration from Russia followed the break-up of the Soviet empire. But Satan continues to oppose every move towards this restoration as, when Russian Jews began arriving in Israel, Saddam Hussein rained down missiles on Haifa and other places during the first Gulf War, a seemingly inexplicable tactic as Israel was not involved in the conflict. But there *is* an explanation: God-haters ultimately attack the Jew, the 'apple of His eye'. The very survival of this people after numerous attempts at genocide over millennia is nothing short of miraculous. The fact that Israel exists as a nation today is clear testament to the existence of the God who acts in history, as he did 3,500 years ago when they escaped from Egypt through the Red Sea, when the waters parted to allow them to flee on dry land before closing in on their enemies. David Ben Gurion, Israel's first Prime Minister, once said: "A Jew who does not believe in miracles is not a realist."

The national restoration to the Lord referred to by Ezekiel, Jeremiah and others is still to come although, as we have seen, thousands of individual Jews have believed in Jesus over the centuries. A turning point was the Six-Day War of June 1967 which brought Jerusalem's Old City back into Israel's hands for the first time in 2,000 years. Perhaps even more significant was the fact that a new spiritual dawn was also breaking. For it was around this time that so-called Messianic fellowships began to appear on the scene. Israeli Jews were starting to recognise Jesus as their Messiah, and these groups have spread far and wide. Though still only representing a small percentage of the populace, they are nevertheless having an influence on national life out of all proportion to their numbers, so that today Jesus is publicly discussed in the nation's media. Their testimony is vibrant and courageous, and in the midst of all the conflict they are demonstrating the beauty of the "one new man" spoken of by the Apostle Paul as Jew and Arab, reconciled through the death and resurrection of Jesus, worship together in congregations throughout the land.

God has an end-time role for both Jews and believing Gentiles. Israel is called to be "a light for the Gentiles" (Isaiah 49.6) and the Gentiles are called to comfort Israel (Isaiah 40.1f). Although Israel's light will ultimately "bring salvation to the ends of the earth", it will also be fulfilled in other practical ways. For example, they have become world leaders in technological innovation, providing components for mobile phones and turning a desert into a garden through their drip system of irrigation, thus filling the world with fruit in fulfilment of ancient prophecies. They are also world leaders in medical breakthroughs and in extending compassion to suffering people, as demonstrated by the way they are often first on the scene of disasters, such as the earthquakes in Haiti, Nepal, Ecuador and Japan. Their doctors even treat the wounded of their enemies as is happening today on their northern border where civil war continues to wreak havoc in Syria. In this way, they are doing what Jesus urged them to do by loving their enemies. They may not all be right with the Lord yet, but they still demonstrate more 'Christian' behaviour as a nation than the rest of us. In addition, they have turned a wasteland into a thriving, modern democracy, giving a say – even in their parliament – to those who seek their destruction. They keep encouraging more immigration to an already crowded tiny strip of land. As for spiritual light, well... they have given us the Bible, God the Father has given us His Son, Jesus – and the people live in 'God's own country.' There is further light to come, as they will take part in the final harvest of the earth (Romans 11.26, Revelation 7 and 14).

God's ultimate purpose for the Jewish people is that they will be a blessing to the nations. Robin Aldridge has an interesting take on this: "The fact that there are tens of thousands of Messianic Jewish people in Israel today has caused God to bless the people around her, so there is a real work of the Holy Spirit taking place in countries like Egypt and Iran. And nearly all the Messianic congregations have a burden to share their faith with their Arab brothers. So there is this real peace process taking place with Jesus at the centre. Many of the Messianic congregations are in fact a mixture of Arabs and Jews worshipping together. At the same time there are also tens of thousands of Muslims coming to faith in the surrounding countries. After all, they are all Semitic people and the promises of God's favour apply to the descendants of Ishmael as well as Isaac."

As for us Gentiles, our role at this time is to comfort the Jews, to pray for them and to proclaim salvation through their Messiah. Actually, our first duty is to preach the gospel (Romans 1.16). Isaiah puts it this way: "Comfort, comfort my people, says your God. Speak tenderly to Jerusalem, and proclaim to her ... that her sin has been paid for..." (Isa 40.1f). Many will still be feeling abandoned by God, especially in light of the Holocaust, saying: “The Lord has forsaken me, the Lord has forgotten me” (Isa 49.14). But we must share the gospel: “How beautiful on the mountains are the feet of those who bring good news… who say to Zion, ‘Your God reigns!’” (Isa 52.7). The prophet also puts it this way: “You who bring good tidings to Zion, go up on a high mountain. You who bring good tidings to Jerusalem, lift up your voice with a shout … say to the towns of Judah, ‘Here is your God!’” (Isa 40.9). So, whether we proclaim this message in Israel, or perhaps through the internet, it needs to be shouted from the rooftops – from a high and holy place. It is the Lord’s call to the Gentile nations: “Say to the Daughter of Zion, ‘See, your Saviour comes!’…” And our message must emphasise the spiritual rather than the material; that we are just passing through this earth, but that the Word of God stands forever (see Isa 40.6-8). We must also pray for Israel. “Pray for the peace of Jerusalem” is the clear call of Psalm 122.6 and Isaiah 62.6f calls us to intercede on her behalf, giving ourselves no rest until God makes her the praise of the earth.

Clearly, the Mandate period was not Britain’s finest hour. But many Jewish people are unaware of our positive contribution to their welfare in times past. They see only carping criticism of their government and broken promises made to their forbears. Now, particularly with the centenary of the Balfour Declaration in mind, we have an opportunity to put that right by reminding the present generation that there have been many Christians in the UK who have consistently shown their love and support for the Jewish people over the years.

Christians called to comfort Israel

It was over seven years ago that my pen was first fired with a new passion. The Lord's still, small voice dropped into my heart, saying: 'I want you to be a helper of Israel'. I was meditating on some chapters from Isaiah during a holiday at the seaside with Linda. It was pouring with rain, so we stayed in to read. The opening words of Chapter 40 (already part-quoted above) washed over me like a sweet-smelling rain shower that brought tears to my eyes: "Comfort, comfort my people, says your God. Speak tenderly to Jerusalem, and proclaim to her that her hard service has been completed, that her sin has been paid for, that she has received from the Lord's hand double for all her sins."

You can read the rest for yourself but, just as the prophet was answering God's call to proclaim the word of the Lord to His people, so on that rainy day I felt a clear command to do the same. It has been an incredible journey since then that has included three wonderful trips to Israel and writing several books. Although born in South Africa and having lived in England for my entire adult life, I almost felt I had come home on those visits. And I guess that was true in view of my Sephardic Jewish ancestry. Anyway, writing this book was another outcome of God speaking to me that cold autumn day on the beautiful Yorkshire coast. As Jews everywhere come under increasing threat from Islam and other anti-Semitic sources, I am here to stand with them as a Christian who is a friend of Israel.

I am sure it won't have escaped your notice that the jihadists are seeking to murder us both – Jews and Christians. The butchering of 21 Coptic Christians on a beach in Libya was just one example of their merciless brutality. Apparently the victims cried out, 'Help me, Jesus!' before their beheadings. It is important to distinguish between those who live in the 'Christian' West and genuine believers who refuse to surrender to intimidation and threats, or appease their opponents for short-term political gain, or cut themselves off from the Hebraic root of their faith.

Islamic terrorists miss the target by miles when they attack cartoonists who mock Mohammed. Journalists enjoy a free press only because of a Judeo-Christian civilisation that encouraged open expression and debate – based on belief in a God who can speak for himself and does not need brutal bodyguards. Many Western scribes these days are in fact enemies of Christianity, and of Israel, as they submit to political correctness and self-censorship in order not to offend certain groups. But they are not afraid of mocking the faith on which their freedom depends. However, I was very encouraged to hear an excerpt from a BBC news program focusing on wounded Syrian soldiers being treated by Israeli doctors, as the BBC does not have a reputation for showing Israel in a positive light.

So I say to Jewish readers: as you comfort others, may you yourselves be comforted, in accordance with the Scriptures. There are Christians standing with you all over the world. Among them are a South African couple I know who told me of a 'divine appointment' they had with a rabbi's wife on a Virgin Atlantic flight. My friends, who live in Port Elizabeth, have a *Care for Israel List*, regularly sending articles about Israel to contacts and calling them to prayer. They also contribute to a charity called DIVOTE, collecting and packing new baby items which get sent on to Israel by a lady in Durban.

For their Christmas Eve flight to see family in the UK, they were moved twice before finally being given bulkhead seats next to the rabbi's wife and her six children. "I got chatting to her and told her how much we loved the nation of Israel and its people and just happened to mention some of the projects that we are involved in, and that there were a number of people in our church who supported Israel," my friend wrote. "She did not realise that there were people like that out there and said she felt 'cleansed from anti-Semitism'.

"Then two weeks ago I got a phone call from the Jewish lady who handles our donations of the baby items who said that a certain rabbi's wife happened to mention that she had met a couple on the plane who supported DIVOTE and that she had cried when I was not looking as she was so touched. How amazing is that! The Lord had given us preferred seating so we could tell his people how much he loves them!"

Also from South Africa comes the remarkable story of when CMJ worker Edith Sher travelled 1,000 miles to address a 70-strong congregation on a guest farm. Since it coincided with Yom Kippur (Israel's Day of Atonement) she decided to speak of how Yeshua – as the atoning sacrifice for our sins – was the perfect fulfilment of this holiest of Jewish days. But, before the meeting convened, a secular Israeli family touring the country rang to request overnight accommodation. The owners, Ina and Hendrik Goosen, warned that a Christian meeting would be taking place. But they didn't mind. In fact, they took part in the proceedings and were overwhelmed by the love for Israel expressed by these believers!

Such support for Israel is in fact a default position for much of the South African church which I believe is why they are experiencing revival as I write. For example, nearly two million people attended a prayer meeting on a farmer's field near the central city of Bloemfontein to pray for a nation stricken by corruption, crime, violence and unemployment. If you bless Israel, you will know blessing yourselves (see Genesis 12.3), and this is clearly the reason why South Africa's Christians are speaking and acting with one voice.

That blessing Israel is a key to revival should come as no surprise to us. After all, the Roman centurion Cornelius, who prayed regularly, helped the poor and loved the Jews, became the means of blessing for the entire Gentile world when the Holy Spirit came upon him and his family through the preaching of the Apostle Peter, once the latter was finally convinced by a powerful vision during which God urged him three times to share the gospel with those he had until then considered 'unclean' (see Acts 10). I imagine this is the same centurion mentioned in Luke's gospel (7.2-5 – Luke also wrote Acts), and sometimes wonder if he is not perhaps the same man who, witnessing the crucifixion, "praised God and said, 'Surely this was a righteous man'" (Luke 23.47).

Like Cornelius, today's Gentiles are called to comfort God's people, to bring good tidings to Zion and say to the towns of Judah, 'Here is your God!' (See Isaiah 40.1-9.)

In addition, we must serve them – help their poor, advocate for them when they are maligned with lies and stand up to be counted with them, which definitely means that we should never get swept up with fashionable campaigns such as the current BDS (Boycott, Divestment and Sanctions) movement basically aimed at delegitimising Israel. We can also facilitate their Aliyah (returning to their homeland) in accordance with Isaiah 49.22: "See, I will beckon to the Gentiles… they will bring your sons in their arms and carry your daughters on their shoulders." It would have been better for Britain if they had done more of this in the 1930s and 40s when Jews were in fear of their lives in Nazi-occupied Europe. For if we refuse to serve them, we put ourselves and our country in grave danger. "For the nation or kingdom that will not serve you will perish; it will be utterly ruined" (Isaiah 60.12). Britain has lost her empire, and much more. The Judeo-Christian ethos on which her greatness was built has been scattered to the winds of destruction as anti-Semitism raises its ugly head once more, even in the heart of the nation's politics. There is an urgent need to repent of our great sin.

We could take a lesson from the Book of Esther, which tells of the beautiful Jewish girl who became Queen to the Persian King Xerxes. But when her uncle and guardian Mordecai heard of a plot to exterminate the Jews, he challenged her with the thought that she may well have been brought to the kingdom "for such a time as this". So she risked her life by approaching the king without being invited, and saved her people as a result. Mordecai had warned his niece: "Do not think that because you are in the king's house you alone of all the Jews will escape. For if you remain silent at this time, relief and deliverance for the Jews will arise from another place, but you and your father's family will perish" (Esther 4.14). The Church is the bride of Christ, and has a duty to love and watch over his people, the Jews, to shepherd them back to their land, and their Lord. If we don't act on their behalf, God will raise up someone else who will, but we will perish. That is a pretty devastating thought. So don't let it happen. You too were called to the kingdom "for such a time as this".

Crombie, Kelvin, *Anzacs, Empires and Israel's Restoration* (Vocational Education & Training Publications)
Crombie, Kelvin, *The Restoration of Israel*, (Nicolayson's, Christ Church, Jerusalem)
Gardner, Charles, *Israel the Chosen*
Gardner, Charles, *Peace in Jerusalem*, Olive Press
Crombie, Kelvin, *A Prophetic Property* (Israel Trust of the Anglican Church, ITAC)
Fisher, Julia, *What is God Doing in Israel?* (Monarch)
Bryson, Bill, *One Summer: America 1927* (Black Swan; Transworld Publishers)
Kendall, R.T., *God Meant it for Good* (Kingsway)
Wright, Fred, *Father, Forgive Us* (Monarch/Olive Press)
Prince, Derek & Lydia, *Appointment in Jerusalem* (Kingsway)
Wurmbrand, Richard *Tortured for Christ* (Release International)
Grubb, Norman, *Rees Howells: Intercessor* (Lutterworth)
Yousef Mosab Hassan with Brackin, Ron, *Son of Hamas* (Tyndale Momentum)
Smith, Lynley, *From Matron to Martyr* (Tate Publishing)
Pawson, David, *Unlocking the Bible* (Collins)
Bryson, Bill, *The Road to Little Dribbling* (Doubleday; Transworld Publishers)
Hames, Paul, *The London Jews Society and the Balfour Declaration* (Olive Press)
Jacob, Alex, *A Synoptic History of Jewish Mission* (Olive Press)
Christian Friends of Israel's *Watching Over Zion* newsletter from David Soakell

See also

Jerusalem News Network (part of Barry Segal's Vision for Israel humanitarian ministry)
Israel Today magazine & online site www.israeltoday.co.il
Friends of Zion Jerusalem Prayer Team International newsletters from Dr Mike Evans
Saltshakers.com – the website of author Steve Maltz

GROUPS SUPPORTING ISRAEL

The following is a list of organisations, mostly with British links, known to the author as supporters of Israel. It is by no means exhaustive: Christians For Israel, The Church's Ministry among Jewish people (CMJ), Christian Friends of Israel, Messianic Testimony, Christian Witness to Israel, Maoz Israel, Bridges for Peace, Vision for Israel & the Joseph Storehouse Trust, Christians United for Israel, the International Christian Embassy of Jerusalem, Conservative Friends of Israel, Labour Friends of Israel, the Emmaus Group, Jews for Jesus, Pardes (a centre of biblical and Hebraic studies linked with Issachar Ministries), Tishrei Bible School – www.tishrei.org – producing on-line courses exploring the Hebraic roots of the Christian faith for use at home or in church groups, Saltshakers (the ministry of author Steve Maltz), Prayer for Israel, the Evangelical Sisterhood of Mary, the Hatikvah Film Trust, Lydia Fellowship International, Revelation TV, Methodist Friends of Israel and United with Israel.

ABOUT THE AUTHOR

Charles Gardner is a 68-year-old Cape Town-born journalist who began his career in Fleet Street as a London correspondent for the *South African Press Association*. He subsequently moved to Yorkshire, where he has been involved in a senior editorial capacity on a number of newspapers over the past 39 years. He has also launched Christian publications, including the evangelistic tabloid *New Life*, and after retirement from full-time work in 2012, signed up as a volunteer with the Church's Ministry among Jewish people (CMJ). He is also author of *Israel the Chosen* (Amazon) and *Peace in Jerusalem* (olivepresspublisher.com). He is married to Linda, 60, who teaches Christianity and Judaism in Doncaster's primary schools, and has four children and nine grandchildren. He is also a regular contributor to www.prophecytoday.uk, *Heart Publications* in the South-East of England, Jerusalem-based *Israel Today* – www.israeltoday.co.il, global news service ASSIST (Aid to Special Saints In Strategic Times), *Gateway News* (an online portal in South Africa) and CMJ's USA and UK websites.